# Raspberry Pi Projects for Kids

Start your own coding adventure with your kids by creating cool and exciting games and applications on the Raspberry Pi

**Daniel Bates**

**[PACKT]** open source
PUBLISHING     community experience distilled

BIRMINGHAM - MUMBAI

# Raspberry Pi Projects for Kids

First published: March 2014

Production Reference: 1180314

Published by Packt Publishing Ltd.
Livery Place
35 Livery Street
Birmingham B3 2PB, UK.

ISBN 978-1-78398-222-6

www.packtpub.com

Cover Image by ©iStock.com/pringletta

# Credits

**Author**

Daniel Bates

**Reviewers**

Georg Bisseling

Colin Deady

Prasanna Gautam

Sungjin Han

Claes Jakobsson

Ian McAlpine

**Acquisition Editors**

Harsha Bharwani

Kunal Parikh

**Content Development Editor**

Mohammed Fahad

**Technical Editors**

Krishnaveni Haridas

Ankita Thakur

**Copy Editors**

Insiya Morbiwala

Kirti Pai

**Project Coordinator**

Mrudula Manjrekar

**Proofreader**

Maria Gould

**Indexer**

Priya Subramani

**Graphics**

Ronak Dhruv

**Production Coordinator**

Komal Ramchandani

**Cover Work**

Komal Ramchandani

# About the Author

**Daniel Bates** is a Computer Science researcher at the University of Cambridge. His day job involves inventing designs for future mobile phone processors, and when he goes home, he likes playing games or working on one of his coding projects (or both!). Daniel has been a volunteer for the Raspberry Pi Foundation since 2011, and is enthusiastic about introducing new people to computing. He has previously written *Instant Minecraft: Pi Edition Coding How-to, Packt Publishing*.

# About the Reviewers

**Georg Bisseling** is a software developer with two decades of experience in many fields as diverse as neural networks, cryptography, radio monitoring, high performance computing, and business intelligence systems. He lives in Bonn, the former capital city of Western Germany.

**Colin Deady** started his career in IT in the late 1990s when he discovered software testing ("They want me to break it?"), having previously fallen in love with computers, thanks to his parents buying a ZX81 and ZX Spectrum+ for him and his brother in the 1980s. He graduated to using an Amiga 1200 in the early 1990s and spent countless hours learning the insides of the operating system. Now, with 14 years of experience in testing, he works as a Test Manager with an emphasis on test automation, extolling the virtues of Agile using Kanban and behavior-driven development to great effect (test early, test often; fix early, fix often). In his spare time, Colin is part of the editorial team for *The MagPi* (www.themagpi.com), a community-written magazine for the Raspberry Pi. With several published articles and having reviewed and edited many more, he has built up extensive knowledge on this tiny platform. He can also be found jointly running *The MagPi* stand at regular Bristol DigiMakers events in the UK, demonstrating things such as a remote control robot arm, a roverbot, and LED display boards, all of which he has programmed in Python on the Raspberry Pi. He currently runs a blog related to all features of the Raspberry Pi at www.rasptut.co.uk.

**Prasanna Gautam** is an engineer who wears many different hats depending on the occasion. He graduated from Trinity College in 2011 and is currently working as a software engineer at ESPN on cool projects. He has worked on building robots that extinguish fires in firefighting contests and robots that autonomously moved around obstacles. He was involved with the **One Laptop Per Child (OLPC)** event in Nepal and is fascinated by educational projects that teach programming and logic to kids. In his free time, Prasanna attempts to play the guitar and make sense of music theory.

**Sungjin Han** likes to ride a bicycle and loves to tinker around on the dark terminal; he also enjoys newly released gadgets and technologies. Now, he is working for a startup in South Korea, looking for some more interesting stuff to dive in to.

**Claes Jakobsson** started his career in the mid-90s and quickly became involved in the open source community, hacking code and organizing stuff in his hometown of Stockholm. Although Perl is his primary focus, he made forays into PostgreSQL, cURL, and other projects. His daytime occupation has been mostly financial systems, but at night, playing with embedded systems, microcontrollers, virtual machines, compilers, and the interest du jour kept the mind at bay. He is a technologist at heart with a mind to share, and he is always eager to see what happens next.

**Ian McAlpine** was first introduced to computers at his school, to the research machine RML-380Z and his Physics teacher's Compukit UK101. That was followed by a Sinclair ZX81 and then a BBC Micro Model A, which he has to this day. That interest resulted in an MEng in Electronic Systems Engineering from Aston University and an MSc in Information Technology from the University of Liverpool. Ian is currently a senior product owner at SAP. The introduction of the Raspberry Pi rekindled his desire to "tinker", but also provided an opportunity to give back to the community. Consequently, Ian is a very active volunteer working on *The MagPi*, a monthly magazine for the Raspberry Pi, which you can read online or download for free from www.themagpi.com.

I would like to thank my darling wife, Louise, and my awesome kids, Emily and Molly, for their patience and support.

# www.PacktPub.com

## Support files, eBooks, discount offers and more

You might want to visit www.PacktPub.com for support files and downloads related to your book.

Did you know that Packt offers eBook versions of every book published, with PDF and ePub files available? You can upgrade to the eBook version at www.PacktPub.com and as a print book customer, you are entitled to a discount on the eBook copy. Get in touch with us at service@packtpub.com for more details.

At www.PacktPub.com, you can also read a collection of free technical articles, sign up for a range of free newsletters and receive exclusive discounts and offers on Packt books and eBooks.

http://PacktLib.PacktPub.com

Do you need instant solutions to your IT questions? PacktLib is Packt's online digital book library. Here, you can access, read and search across Packt's entire library of books.

## Why Subscribe?

- Fully searchable across every book published by Packt
- Copy and paste, print and bookmark content
- On demand and accessible via web browser

## Free Access for Packt account holders

If you have an account with Packt at www.PacktPub.com, you can use this to access PacktLib today and view nine entirely free books. Simply use your login credentials for immediate access.

# Table of Contents

**Preface**                                                                    **1**

**Chapter 1: Getting Started with the Raspberry Pi**                           **5**

**Materials needed**                                                           **6**
  Power supply                                                                  6
  Storage                                                                       6
  Input                                                                         7
  Video                                                                         7
  Network                                                                       8
**Preparing the SD card**                                                      **8**
**Starting up the Raspberry Pi**                                              **10**
**Using your Raspberry Pi**                                                   **13**
  The command line                                                            13
  Updating and installing new software                                        14
  Other uses for Raspberry Pi                                                 15
  Troubleshooting                                                             16
**Summary**                                                                   **17**

**Chapter 2: Making Your Own Angry Birds Game**                               **19**

**Scratch**                                                                   **20**
  Hello world!                                                                21
  Code tour                                                                   22
**Creating a character**                                                      **23**
**Creating a level**                                                          **25**
**Moving the character**                                                      **26**
  Initialization                                                              26
  Moving with the keyboard                                                    27
  Launch!                                                                     28
  Flight                                                                      30

**Adding physics**    **30**
  Gravity    31
  Bouncing    31
  Ending the game    32
**Scoring**    **33**
**Extensions**    **35**
**Summary**    **35**

**Chapter 3: Testing Your Speed**    **37**
**Materials needed**    **37**
**Creating the game controller**    **38**
  The controller base    39
  Adding buttons    39
  Connecting to the Raspberry Pi    42
**Python**    **43**
**Coding the game**    **45**
  Random behavior    45
  Using the controller    46
  Adding a time limit    48
  Bringing it all together    49
**Complete code listing**    **50**
**The keyboard version**    **52**
**What's next?**    **53**
**Summary**    **53**

**Chapter 4: Making an Interactive Map of Your City**    **55**
**Hello world!**    **56**
  Tkinter    56
  Writing the program    56
**Getting a map**    **58**
  No Internet? No problem!    58
  Google Maps    59
  Generating the address    60
  Downloading the image    61
  Using the image    62
**Adding markers**    **63**
  Detecting mouse clicks    64
  Reacting to mouse clicks    64
**Adding labels**    **66**
  Basic labels    66
  Pop-up windows    66

**Code listing**   **69**

**Extensions**   **71**

  Layout   72

  Additional widgets   72

    Checkbutton   72

    Frame and LabelFrame   73

    Listbox   73

    Menu   73

    Menubutton   74

    Message   74

    OptionMenu   74

    Radiobutton   75

    Scale   75

    Spinbox   75

**Summary**   **76**

**Index**   **77**

# Preface

After introducing the Raspberry Pi computer and showing you how to set it up, this book guides you and your kids through three separate mini projects. Each project is fun, visual, and has plenty of scope for personalization. By the end of this book, you will understand and be able to use two different programming languages, and will be able to use them to build creative programs of your own.

## What this book covers

*Chapter 1, Getting Started with the Rasberry Pi*, will show you what a Raspberry Pi is, and how you can get one set up and ready to use.

*Chapter 2, Making Your Own Angry Birds Game*, will teach you how to make your very own computer game using the Scratch programming language.

*Chapter 3, Testing Your Speed*, will guide you on how to connect lights and switches to your Raspberry Pi to create a physical game, controlled by your computer code. This chapter introduces the Python programming language.

*Chapter 4, Making an Interactive Map of Your City*, will teach you more about Python, and will show you how to access Google Maps to create a personal map of your area.

## What you need for this book

All projects in this book require a Raspberry Pi and all the necessary peripherals (listed at the beginning of *Chapter 1, Getting Started with the Rasberry Pi*). *Chapter 3, Testing Your Speed*, adds simple electronic components to the Raspberry Pi, and again, these are listed at the beginning of that chapter.

# Who this book is for

This book is designed to help adults and children jump into creative coding, using the Raspberry Pi. You will need patience, a sense of adventure, and a vivid imagination!

# Conventions

In this book, you will find a number of styles of text that distinguish between different kinds of information. Here are some examples of these styles, and an explanation of their meaning.

Code words in text are shown as follows: "This script waits until it receives the launch message."

A block of code is set as follows:

```
def count(maximum):
    value = 0
    while value < maximum:
        value = value + 1
        print "value =", value
```

**New terms** and **important words** are shown in bold. Words that you see on the screen, in menus or dialog boxes for example, appear in the text like this: "Select **Raspbian** and click on **Install**".

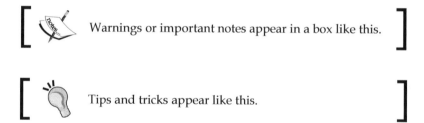

Warnings or important notes appear in a box like this.

Tips and tricks appear like this.

# Reader feedback

Feedback from our readers is always welcome. Let us know what you think about this book—what you liked or may have disliked. Reader feedback is important for us to develop titles that you really get the most out of.

To send us general feedback, simply send an e-mail to feedback@packtpub.com, and mention the book title through the subject of your message.

If there is a topic that you have expertise in and you are interested in either writing or contributing to a book, see our author guide on www.packtpub.com/authors.

# Customer support

Now that you are the proud owner of a Packt book, we have a number of things to help you to get the most from your purchase.

# Downloading the example code

You can download the example code files for all Packt books you have purchased from your account at http://www.packtpub.com. If you purchased this book elsewhere, you can visit http://www.packtpub.com/support and register to have the files e-mailed directly to you.

# Downloading the color images of this book

We also provide you a PDF file that has color images of the screenshots/diagrams used in this book. The color images will help you better understand the changes in the output. You can download this file from: http://www.packtpub.com/sites/default/files/downloads/2226OS_ColoredImages.pdf

# Errata

Although we have taken every care to ensure the accuracy of our content, mistakes do happen. If you find a mistake in one of our books—maybe a mistake in the text or the code—we would be grateful if you would report this to us. By doing so, you can save other readers from frustration and help us improve subsequent versions of this book. If you find any errata, please report them by visiting http://www.packtpub.com/support, selecting your book, clicking on the **errata submission form** link, and entering the details of your errata. Once your errata are verified, your submission will be accepted and the errata will be uploaded to our website, or added to any list of existing errata, under the Errata section of that title.

# Piracy

Piracy of copyright material on the Internet is an ongoing problem across all media. At Packt, we take the protection of our copyright and licenses very seriously. If you come across any illegal copies of our works, in any form, on the Internet, please provide us with the location address or website name immediately so that we can pursue a remedy.

Please contact us at copyright@packtpub.com with a link to the suspected pirated material.

We appreciate your help in protecting our authors, and our ability to bring you valuable content.

# Questions

You can contact us at questions@packtpub.com if you are having a problem with any aspect of the book, and we will do our best to address it.

# 1
# Getting Started with the Raspberry Pi

In the mid-2000s, some of the staff at the University of Cambridge noticed that there were fewer and fewer students applying to study Computer Science each year, and that they had less and less experience. Something had to be done. The answer was the Raspberry Pi — a small, inexpensive computer that makes programming as accessible and as much fun as possible. The idea is that students can play with the Raspberry Pi during their spare time, and in the process, learn valuable core Computer Science skills. Since its creation, many other groups have discovered how useful the Raspberry Pi can be, including schools, adults who want to brush up on their skills with technology, and electronics hobbyists.

This chapter describes how to get a Raspberry Pi computer up and running. Once this is done, the Pi behaves just like any other ordinary computer, and is capable of standard tasks such as browsing the web and playing games. We will learn in later chapters that the Raspberry Pi is also capable of performing some tasks which ordinary computers can't do. The following figure shows a Raspberry Pi board:

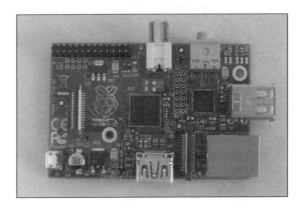

# Materials needed

This book assumes that a Raspberry Pi *Model B* is used, with its two USB ports and network connection (shown in the preceding figure). *Model A* (with one USB port and no network connection) will also work, but a USB hub (described later) will be needed to allow both a keyboard and a mouse to be used at the same time.

Along with a Raspberry Pi computer, you will need the following peripherals. In order to keep costs down, the Raspberry Pi was designed to work with devices that people already owned; so you may find many of these components around your house already. Just make sure they're not in use before you take them!

 http://elinux.org/RPi_VerifiedPeripherals is a useful website for checking whether a particular device will work with the Raspberry Pi.

# Power supply

The Raspberry Pi requires a Micro-USB connection (shown in the following figure), which is capable of supplying at least 700 mA (or 0.7 A) at 5V. Power supplies that can provide 1000 mA and more are available (and will be more reliable), but your chosen supply must give exactly 5 V. Most standard mobile phone chargers are suitable, and have their capabilities written on them, so you can check. Do not attempt to power your Pi from a USB port of another computer or hub as they are often incapable of supplying the required current.

# Storage

The operating system and all files are stored on a standard SD card (shown in the following figure), which you may find in a digital camera. You will need at least 4 GB of space (preferably 8 GB+). The Raspberry Pi Foundation sells very affordable 8 GB SD cards with the operating system preinstalled at http://swag.raspberrypi. org/. You will also need a way to write data to an SD card from another computer. Many computers have built-in SD writers, but it is possible to buy USB dongles which do the job too.

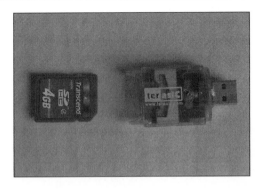

# Input

For inputs, we will use a USB keyboard and mouse (as shown in the following figures):

# Video

We will use a monitor or a television with HDMI or DVI input, and a video cable connected from the Pi's HDMI port to the screen's input, as shown in the following figures. It is possible to connect to an older VGA or composite screen, but this is more complicated (refer to the *Verified Peripherals* link at the start of this section).

# Network

An Internet connection is not essential, but is very useful as it allows you to work directly on the Pi. The easiest approach is to use a wired Ethernet connection. It is also possible to use a USB Wi-Fi dongle. You will need a powered USB hub to provide additional USB ports, as shown in the following images:

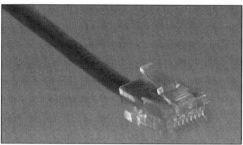 

You may also like to put your Raspberry Pi in a case to protect it, though this is certainly not necessary. There are many different companies that make many different styles, so choose one that suits you, or you could even make your own from Lego or card!

# Preparing the SD card

The first thing we need to do is put an operating system on the SD card using another computer. You can buy SD cards with preinstalled software, but doing it yourself guarantees that you get the latest updates and is also a useful learning experience. These instructions assume that you are using a computer running Microsoft Windows or Mac OS X; if you are using another operating system or having difficulties, detailed instructions are available online at `http://www.raspberrypi.org/downloads`.

There is a *Troubleshooting* section at the end of the chapter if you get stuck. We can prepare the SD card by performing the following steps:

1. Download the SD association's formatting tool, SD Formatter, from `http://www.sdcard.org/downloads/formatter_4/`.

2. Download the latest version of the NOOBS (offline install) operating system collection from `http://www.raspberrypi.org/downloads`.

3. Insert the SD card into the SD card writer (shown in the following image):

4. If the SD card writer is separate from your computer, plug it in.

5. Install and run the SD Formatter (shown in the following screenshot). Select the SD card you just inserted and click on **Format**. In this example, the SD card is drive G, but this will vary from computer to computer.

 Make absolutely sure that you have the right SD card selected. All the data will be lost from the formatted card.

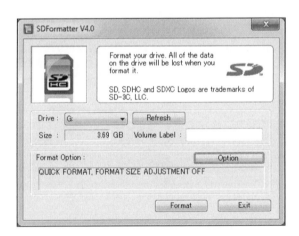

6. Extract the contents of the NOOBS ZIP file to the SD card. The way this is done will vary depending on what software you have installed, but will typically involve double-clicking on NOOBS.zip, clicking on **Extract** or **Extract to...**, and selecting the SD card as the destination. There is a lot to extract, so this will take a few minutes to complete.

7.  Safely remove/eject the SD card and take it out of the SD writer, as shown in the following figure:

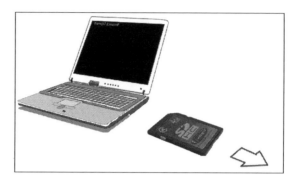

# Starting up the Raspberry Pi

Now we can prepare the Raspberry Pi to start up for the first time. Place it securely on a desk or in a case. Make sure it is not in danger of falling on the floor, and do not rest it on top of the bag inside which it comes. We can start up the Rasberry Pi by performing the following steps:

1.  Plug the SD card, screen, keyboard, and mouse into the Raspberry Pi. Also plug in the Internet cable if you have one, as shown in the following figure:

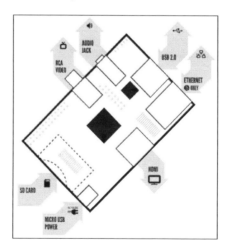

2.  Plug the power cable into the Raspberry Pi. The red power light should come on, and the green Activity light should flash occasionally.

3.  If necessary, adjust the screen settings to display the images from the Raspberry Pi's input.

4. You should see a selection of operating systems for you to install (refer to the following screenshot), each with a short description. This book relies on you having Raspbian installed, so select **Raspbian** and click on **Install**. You can always come back and select a different operating system later; I will explain how you can do this in the next section.

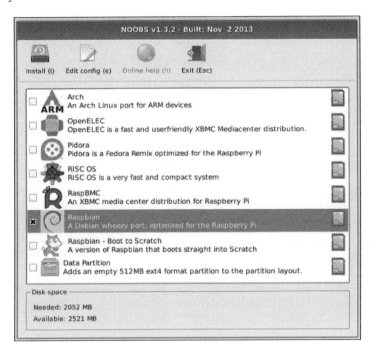

5. Wait. Operating systems are quite large, so the installation will take a few minutes. You can sit back and read some of the tips shown to you or read the next few steps in this book.

6. When the installation has completed, you should see a blue screen with a final list of options (shown in the following screenshot). This is the **Raspberry Pi Software Configuration Tool**. Most things should be set up the way we want them, but there are two useful settings to be changed. Select **Enable Boot to Desktop/Scratch** using the arrow keys and press *Enter*. Select the **Desktop Log in** option, and press *Enter*. You should now be back at the main menu. Next, select **Internationalisation Options** and choose your preferred language and keyboard layout. Use the right arrow key to move to **Finish** and press *Enter*. You can return to this menu any time by typing sudo raspi-config as a command line (refer to the next section for details).

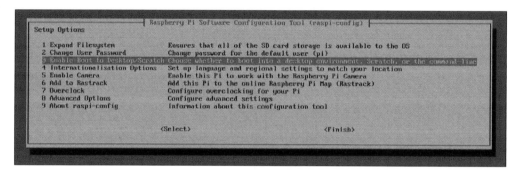

7. After a minute or so, the Raspberry Pi should finish rebooting, and you should see the Raspberry Pi desktop (shown in the following screenshot). This may be familiar to you. You can double-click on the icons to start programs, or select from a menu. We will mainly be using Scratch and Python in this book, but take a minute to explore what's available to you. In particular, there are several **Python Games**. These are the sorts of things that are possible after a little programming practice.

# Using your Raspberry Pi

Now that your Raspberry Pi is up and running, you'll want to know how to keep it working properly and how to customize it to suit your needs.

## The command line

Most of the time, it will be possible to do what you want to do using the mouse by clicking on different parts of the screen; however, at some point, you might find the need to use the command line, as shown in the following screenshot:

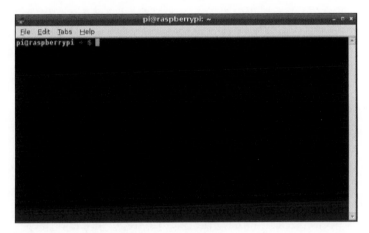

The command line is a completely text-based way of controlling a computer, and can be used to do just about anything that can be done by clicking and more. It is available on almost all computers, but is usually hidden away. Some computer users prefer using the command line because they can type faster than they can click the mouse!

Here is a very quick overview of some common commands. Open a command line by double-clicking on the **LXTerminal** icon on the desktop, and try these out. You will need to press *Enter* to inform the Raspberry Pi that your command has been executed. A longer introduction, including information on how to watch a movie in the command line, can be found online at http://www.techradar.com/news/computing/pc/1161712.

- ls: This lists directory contents. (*Directory* is Linux's word for a folder.) This command will list all the files and directories available to you in the current directory.

- `cd <directory name>`: This changes the directory and allows you to move into another directory, so you can see its contents in the same way that double-clicking on a directory icon moves you into that directory. You can move through multiple levels of directories in one go by separating the directory names with /, and you can go up to the parent directory (the directory that contains the current directory) using the special . . directory name.

- `man <program name>`: This opens the manual and brings up lots of information about a particular program, including what it does and how to use it. It is very useful if you forget how to use something! Try `man ls` to see some advanced information about the `ls` command we tried earlier, and press *q* to quit. You can scroll through the information using the arrow keys or the Space bar.

- `<program name> [extra information]`: This starts the program, and optionally passes some extra information to it. Try typing in `scratch` to start the Scratch program (we'll cover more about this in the next chapter); or, if you are connected to the Internet, navigate to `midori www.raspberrypi.org` to open the Midori web browser and go straight to the Raspberry Pi home page.

- *Tab*: This key automatically completes a word. Even if you have not completely typed in the name of a program or file or folder, try pressing *Tab*. If there is only one option available that begins with the letters you have typed so far, the whole word will be completed for you. If there are multiple options (or none), nothing will change; you can press *Tab* again to display a list of possibilities.

# Updating and installing new software

The Raspberry Pi is an unusual sort of computer, so if you want to install a program, you either need to download a version that is specifically for the Raspberry Pi, or use Raspbian's package system.

A package is a program or a part of a program, and many versions of Linux (including Raspbian) maintain a list of all compatible packages, making it easy to keep all of your software up to date. You can update to the latest version of this list if you have an Internet connection by typing `sudo apt-get update` in the command line.

Be very careful when using the sudo command. It forces the Raspberry Pi to do exactly what you tell it to do, without checking to make sure that the command is sensible. The command is useful in situations like this, where we want to make changes to the installed programs, but it also allows you to delete essential files. Double check your spelling before continuing.

You can search for available packages with keywords using the `apt-cache search <keywords>` command. Try `apt-cache search game`, for example, to see a list of the free games available. You could even try installing one (XBubble is good, for example). The name of the package is the first word of the line, and you can install a package using `sudo apt-get install <package name>`.

To update all the installed packages to the latest available version, type `sudo apt-get upgrade`.

# Other uses for Raspberry Pi

Although the Raspberry Pi was designed to get people interested in computing, its cost and power make sure that it is also popular for other reasons. Since the Raspberry Pi is a general-purpose computer, it is capable of everything a traditional computer can do, but perhaps a little slower. There is a web browser (Midori), word processors, and web servers that are available. A common use case is similar to a media center, to watch films and view pictures.

There are many different operating systems included within the NOOBS package. You can see them if you click on **Shift** when the Raspberry Pi first starts to boot, as shown in the following screenshot:

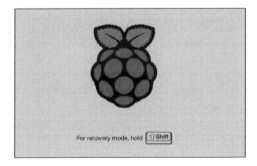

This will take you back to the list you saw earlier when you started your Raspberry Pi for the first time. Each operating system comes with a short description. There are a couple of different flavors of Linux, the very fast RISC OS, and two different media centers, OpenELEC and Raspbmc.

If you want to try one of these operating systems, make sure you first back up all of your data as it will be erased when the new operating system is installed.

# Troubleshooting

One of the main strengths of the Raspberry Pi is its fantastic community. If you ever have any difficulties, consider stopping by the Raspberry Pi forums at `http://www.raspberrypi.org/forum/`. Your question may have already been asked; if not, there are thousands of enthusiastic Pi owners on hand to help. The following are the most common issues:

- **My Raspberry Pi doesn't boot – only the red power light shows**: This suggests that the SD card was not written correctly. Try following the instructions again, and if that fails, try a new SD card.

- **My Raspberry Pi randomly restarts by itself**: This is usually because the Pi is not receiving enough power. Double check that your power supply is capable of supplying at least 700 mA (0.7A) at 5V. This should be written somewhere on the supply. Perhaps you can try upgrading to a 1000 mA (1.0A) supply if you continue to have problems. Also, make sure that you do not have particularly power-hungry peripherals plugged into your Raspberry Pi. For example, some Wi-Fi dongles and keyboards with very bright LEDs can cause problems.

- **I can't enter my password in the login screen**: Nothing is displayed when the password is entered (not even stars) to minimize the information that others can gain from seeing the screen. It is likely that the keys are still being recognized; try typing in the whole password blindly and pressing *Enter*.

- **The display does not fill my screen or extends beyond the edges**: This is because of overscan settings. Many old televisions had cabinets that overlapped a part of the screen, so images were given black borders to ensure that no part of the picture was lost. Many modern monitors, however, do not have this problem, so the black bars are just a nuisance. First try enabling or disabling the overscan settings by typing `sudo raspi-config` at a command line and selecting the appropriate option. If this still does not work, search on the Internet for `Raspberry Pi overscan troubleshooting` for detailed guides.

- **I can't see anything at all on the screen**: If the Pi is definitely on and the OK/ACT light is lit or flashing, try pressing *1*, *2*, *3*, or *4* on your keyboard to select different video modes.

# Summary

In this chapter, we learned how to connect up a Raspberry Pi computer, write its operating system to an SD card, and start everything up. We learned that the Raspberry Pi is capable of doing everything a normal computer can do (and more), and that it is targeted at programming.

In the next chapter, we will use one of the provided programming languages, Scratch, to create our own version of Angry Birds.

# 2
# Making Your Own Angry Birds Game

In this chapter, we are going to make our own version of the popular Angry Birds game. What's more, when we're finished, we will be able to add all sorts of new rules and enemies to keep the game fresh. The following screenshot shows a completed version of our game:

If you haven't played Angry Birds before, here's a quick description of how the game works. The player launches a bird through the air using a slingshot and attempts to hit all of the pigs at the other end of the level. In order to make things more challenging, the pigs are often hidden behind hills or inside flimsy buildings that the player must knock down.

By creating our own version of the game, we have the freedom to change whatever we like. We can change the level design, decrease gravity, fire the bird faster (or bee, in our case), change all of the characters, and add new power-ups and prizes. The sky is the limit!

# Scratch

In this chapter, we will use Scratch to create our game. Scratch is a programming language that has been specially designed to make animations and games with ease. Scratch Version 1.4 comes as standard with the Raspberry Pi but is also available on other computers. You can download it from `http://scratch.mit.edu/` if you ever want to play your game away from your Raspberry Pi. Start up Scratch by double-clicking on its icon on the desktop (it should have the picture of a cartoon cat). The following screenshot shows the Scratch layout:

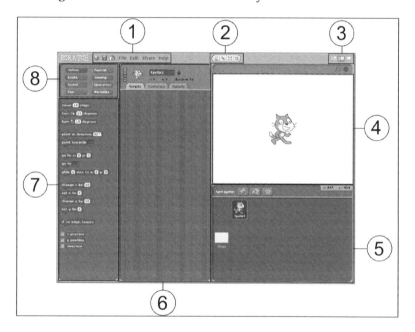

The following are its main sections:

- **Menu (1)**: This is where the options are to save and load your projects. If you ever want inspiration to code for projects, take a look at the provided examples by navigating to **File** | **Open** | **Examples**. Remember to save and back up your progress regularly!

- **Sprite controls** (2): Every picture in the game is called a sprite. These buttons allow you to copy, remove, grow, and shrink sprites. To use them, click on the button you want, and then click on the sprite you want to affect.

- **Screen layout** (3): Choose between a small Stage, a large Stage, and a fullscreen game. The small Stage is better for smaller screens as it allows more space for code.

- **Stage** (4): This is where you will see the effects of all your programming.

- **Sprite list** (5): All of the sprites in your project are shown here, and you can easily add new pictures or change existing ones.

- **Script area** (6): Each sprite has a number of scripts attached to it, and they are shown in this area. Each script is a short piece of code that controls how the sprite behaves.

- **Blocks** (7): Each block is a programming command that can be connected to other blocks (like a jigsaw) to create scripts. Drag a block into the script area to use it, and then drop it next to another block in the script area to join the two.

- **Block types** (8): The blocks are separated into eight different categories, each having different roles in your programs.

# Hello world!

Let's create a very simple program to show how easy it is to produce a visible result. From the **Motion** block type, drag a **turn 15 degrees** block into the script area (this example uses the clockwise turn block), and do the same for the "**when the green flag clicked**" and "**forever**" steps from the **Control** section. Connect them together by dragging one block close to the other. You should see a white highlight where the block needs to be placed. Release the mouse button and the block will snap into place. Click on the green flag present at the top-right corner of the screen to run the program.

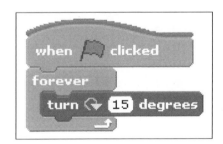

You should see the cat rotating. Your script should also be highlighted to show that it is active. You can change the rotation amount to any number you like to see the cat spin faster or slower—click on **15,** seen in the preceding code block, and type in a new number. You can even choose a negative number, and the cat will spin in the opposite direction. You could also try adding other types of motion blocks within the **forever** block. Click on the red stop sign in the top-right corner to stop your program.

This is how the Raspberry Pi understands your program and knows what to do. It understands that the script should start when the green flag is clicked. As soon as this has happened, it moves on to the next block, **forever**. Everything inside the **forever** block will execute repeatedly until you tell it to stop. In this case, we have told the Raspberry Pi that we want to continuously rotate the cat, and this is what we see. You can see that no blocks can be attached at the bottom of the **forever** block. If something keeps going forever, no later commands will ever run.

# Code tour

There are several types of code blocks available if you want to continue experimenting before we start on the game. A full description can be found online at `http://info.scratch.mit.edu/Support/Reference_Guide_1.4`. A quick tour of the code blocks is as follows:

- **Motion**: This allows us to control where a sprite is on the screen and in which direction it is facing. Its options include rotating, moving to any position, and moving in the direction that the sprite is facing.

- **Control**: This allows us to choose when other blocks of code should run. In the preceding example, we saw how to decide when a script should start and how to repeat a block; however, it is also possible to execute a block only if some condition is true.

- **Looks**: These enable us to decide what a sprite will look like. Each sprite can have multiple images or **costumes** associated with it, and these blocks can be used to switch between them. It is also possible for the sprites to talk or change in size or color.

- **Sensing**: This enables us to allow a sprite to detect its surroundings. We will use it later to work out when a bird in the game hits something.

- **Sound**: This enables us to play sound. You can add new sounds from the **Sounds** tab in the script area.

- **Operators**: These are simple mathematical functions, such as add and subtract. Note that some of the blocks are of different shapes; they show which blocks fit together and will be important later.

- **Pen**: This enables us to allow a sprite to draw a line to show where it has been.

- **Variables**: These allow us to give names to pieces of information so they can be accessed from multiple places. As an example, we will create a variable to hold the game score.

# Creating a character

To start our game, we will need a character to fling through the air. Angry Birds, of course, used birds as its main characters, but we can use whatever we like.

At the top of the sprite list, you should see the three buttons shown in the previous screenshot. The first lets you draw your own character, the second lets you use an existing image (including a wide range of images included with Scratch), and the third gives you a random image from Scratch's selection.

If you click on the first button, you will be shown the following window; it has plenty of easy-to-use options for creating your own drawings. Hover your mouse cursor over any of the buttons to see what they do.

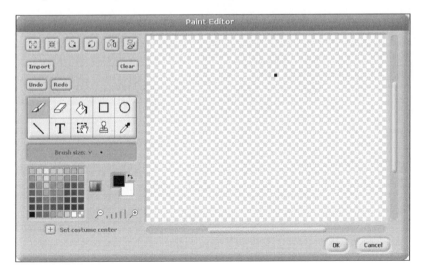

The second button brings up a fairly standard file explorer with lots of neatly categorized images. This is the option I will use, but feel free to do something different.

Once you have drawn or selected a sprite, click on **OK** to add it to the game. If you choose not to use the default cat character, right-click on it in the sprite list and click on **Delete** (this will also delete any code you have created for the cat). You can navigate to **Edit | Undelete** to bring the cat and its code back.

Now that you have a main character, drag it within the Stage to roughly where you think will be a good starting position, and resize it by clicking on the shrink button in the sprite controls and then repeatedly clicking on the sprite. I suggest making the sprite quite small so there is plenty of room around it to fly. Now would also be a good time to give your character a name—there is a textbox at the top of the script area that should say something similar to Sprite 2, which you can change to whatever you like.

Your screen should now look something like the following image but with your own character instead of the bee that I have used:

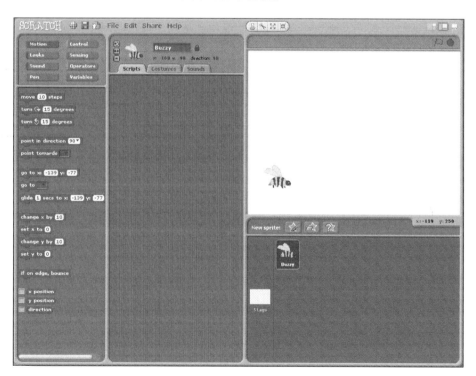

# Creating a level

Now, let's make the game look a little more interesting by adding some scenery with the following steps:

1.  At the left of the sprite list, you'll see a white rectangle called Stage. Click on it and then select the **Backgrounds** tab in the script area. Again, you have the option of drawing your own background or using a pre-existing image, but this time, I recommend creating your own so that you can make the level fun to play.

2.  Click on the **Edit** button. Try to keep your background as simple as possible; it will be easier to add extra objects (for example, the ground, trees, and clouds) as additional sprites later because then you will be able to move them around more easily. It is perhaps easiest to simply fill the background with a solid sky blue color (and maybe some distant mountains).

3.  Now back in the Sprite list, create sprites for all of the scenery you want in your game. At minimum, this will be the ground, but you can add all sorts of little details. With each sprite you create, remember to position it on the Stage, make sure it is the size you want, and give it a descriptive name. Remember that you can duplicate sprites using the left button in the **Sprite Control** area. When you have finished, you might be left with something like the following screenshot:

I have put a hill in the middle of the level to make it more challenging to hit the enemies on the right-hand side of the screen.

When you are happy with your level design, draw a picture of a slingshot and add it to the left-hand side of the Stage. Give it the name `Slingshot` so we are able to find it easily later on. Your Scratch window should now look as follows:

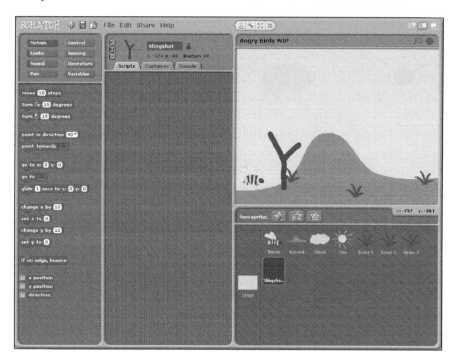

# Moving the character

Now, let's start adding some code and making the game interactive! In this section, we'll do everything necessary to launch our main character using the slingshot.

# Initialization

The first thing we want to do is make sure the position of our main character resets every time we start the game. Click on the main character and create the following script in the script area:

The code snippet states that when the green flag is clicked, the current sprite (the main character) will move to the same position as the slingshot.

Test that your code works by clicking on the green flag. You should see your character jumping to the same position as the slingshot. You may find that the character is behind the slingshot; if you would prefer for it to be in front, simply click on it on the Stage and drag it a short distance. Interacting with any sprite in this way will put it on top of all other sprites.

# Moving with the keyboard

Now, let's allow the player to move the character around using the keyboard so that they can aim their shot. We are mostly going to be making use of this code block (from the **Sensing** section) but with different keys:

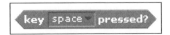

Before you read any further in this book, take a minute to have a look around the available code blocks. Can you find any useful blocks that we could combine with this block to move a sprite up, down, left, or right? This block is a strange shape; how can we connect it with the motion blocks?

There are actually a few different ways to do this, but in this book, we will use the following code block:

Hopefully, this looks fairly sensible to you. If the left arrow key is pressed, do *something*. That *something* may be a bit confusing, however, so here's a quick explanation.

The position of every sprite on the screen is given by two numbers (or coordinates). The x coordinate tells you how far left or right the sprite is, and the y coordinate tells you how far up or down the sprite is. The center of the Stage is at (0,0), that is, both the x and y coordinates are zero. The x coordinate increases from left to right and the y coordinate increases from bottom to top. You can see the current coordinates of any sprite underneath its name in the script area, and the coordinates of the mouse are shown just under the Stage.

Since we want to move left when the left arrow key is pressed, we have to change x by a negative amount. In this case, it has the same effect as subtracting 5.

We will need one of these code blocks for each arrow key:

- The left arrow key should change x by -5
- The right arrow key should change x by 5
- The up arrow key should change y by 5
- The down arrow key should change y by -5

Finally, since we want the player to be able to press each button multiple times to continue adjusting their position, we need to put all of these blocks inside one big **forever** block. The **forever** block should be connected at the bottom of the existing script so the player can adjust the character's position after the position has been reset. Your code should now look as follows:

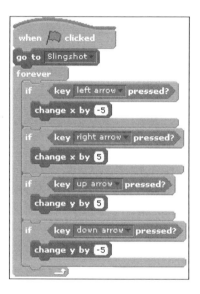

Once again, test your code out by clicking on the green flag. You should be able to move your character around by pressing the various arrow keys.

# Launch!

Now that we've got the character in the right position, let's launch it! First, let's think about what we want to happen when the launch happens. We want to stop the player moving the character (so they can't cheat), and instead, we want to start moving it with a speed and direction dependent on how far from the slingshot the player is.

Since we are moving into a new phase of the game, it is a good idea to use a separate script when we launch. This will help keep each script relatively small and manageable. Add the following code to the **forever** block, where all of your other keyboard-handling blocks are, as follows:

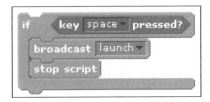

Here, **launch** is the name of a message. When the space key is pressed, launch is sent to all of the other scripts, and if any of them are waiting for that particular message, they will start to run. We also stop the current script so that we stop repeatedly checking which keys are being pressed and the player can't continue to move the character around.

Before we create the second script, we want to be able to calculate how fast to fling the character. To do this, we are going to store the speed in a variable. Variables allow us to store one value each and can be shared between different scripts. In this case, we're using a number, but variables can also store text. We are actually going to use two variables to store the speed: one for up-down speed and the other for left-right speed. The reasons for this will become clear later.

Click on **Variables** and then on **Make a variable**. The following window should pop up. Call your variable x speed, and make sure it is valid only for this sprite. Then do the same to create another variable called y speed. You can choose whether or not a variable is shown on the Stage by clicking on the little box next to it in the code block area.

# Flight

Now that we have these variables, we can create the second script, which will control our flight through the air. The code for this is shown in the following screenshot. It's a little complicated, but try to work out what it does as you build the script up in the script area. I'll explain how it works shortly. (For the two long blocks that are almost identical, it is possible to create one, then right-click on it and duplicate it to save effort in creating the second one.)

The preceding script waits until it receives the **launch** message from the first script. Only then does it start. We set the **x speed** variable to a value that is relative to the distance between the character and the slingshot. I divide the value by **20** to make sure that the flight isn't too fast, but you may prefer a different value here. We then do exactly the same to compute the **y speed** value. Once the speed has been computed, we repeatedly move the object according to our speed.

We're now in a good place to test if everything is working. Click on the green flag, move around, and then launch using the Space bar. You should see your character fly in a straight line across the screen. You may want to try launching from different positions to see how this affects your speed and direction.

One thing that you may have noticed is that your character flies directly through the middle of the slingshot, not the part that it should actually be fired from. This is easy to fix. Click on **Slingshot** in the sprite list, choose the **Costumes** tab in the script area, click on **Edit**, and click on **Set costume center**. You can now drag the crosshairs around to choose a more sensible launch position. Once you have finished, click on **OK**. The slingshot will probably need repositioning on the Stage, but your character's flight should now follow a better path.

# Adding physics

The next thing for us to do is to give our character a more interesting flight path. The game would be too easy (and no fun) if we just flew in a straight line through all the obstacles.

# Gravity

First, let's add some gravity. Gravity has the effect of pulling objects down towards the ground. How can we model gravity in our game? The answer lies in the way we split our speed into both **x speed** and **y speed**. Gravity will only affect **y speed**, our speed in the up-down direction, so we can leave **x speed** as it is. Since the y coordinate increases as we move up but gravity pulls us down, we want gravity to keep subtracting a small amount from the **y speed**. Add the following code block inside the **forever** block of your second script:

Try out the game now. You should arc through the air until you hit one of the edges of the screen. You may tweak the number in this code block if you wish; a more negative number will give stronger gravity. What happens if the number is positive?

# Bouncing

Next, we'll make something more interesting happen if we hit the edge of the screen. As always, there are several options available, but I am going to suggest bouncing off the edges. When we bounce, we want to have the same speed but travel in the opposite direction. When we hit either of the side edges, we want our left-right direction to change, and when we hit the top or bottom edges, we want our up-down direction to change. If there is an **if on edge, bounce** block in the **Motion** section, but it can have some unexpected effects in the game. Add it inside the **forever** block to see the effects, if you like, but remember to remove it again before continuing.

Instead, we'll write our own code to handle bouncing. Add the following code inside the **forever** block:

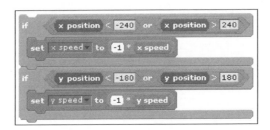

All we're doing here is checking the current position to see if it is at an edge and then reversing the direction. The numbers **240** and **180** come from the width and height of the Stage, respectively, and multiplying by **-1** is a good way to keep the speed the same but reverse the direction.

Have another test of the game. Your character should bounce around the screen in smooth, curved paths.

# Ending the game

The problem is that you bounce around forever. We want the bouncing to stop at some point, and a good time to do this is when the character hits the ground. This is easy to do in Scratch with the following code:

Add this inside the `forever` block, and the script will end when the character sprite hits the ground sprite (you will need to choose the name of the sprite that you used for the ground). Since this script is in control of the character's movement, ending the script ends the movement, which is what we wanted.

Give your physics a final test by playing the game. Your character should fly through the air while being pulled downwards by gravity, bounce off the edges of the screen, and stop when it hits the ground. Your second script should now look as follows:

# Scoring

Now that our main character can be launched properly, it's time to give the player something to aim at. In Angry Birds, there are pigs, but we can have anything we like. Draw a new sprite or use an existing one in the same way we created the main character earlier. I am going to use a pre-made shark in this example. Resize the sprite and put it in a good position.

Do you remember how we checked to see when the main character hit the ground? We're going to need to do something very similar here to detect when an enemy is hit by the main character. The following is the main piece of code to detect collisions, and inside it, we're going to put all of the effects we want to happen when the enemy is hit. Make sure the enemy sprite is selected when you create this script—it controls the enemy's behavior and not the main character's. Note that we're using **forever if** rather than just **if** as we want to keep checking for collisions. Buzzy is the name of the sprite for my main bee character.

If everything has been done right, when an enemy is hit, the following events occur:

- The enemy disappears
- The score is updated
- The script for this enemy stops—we don't care about any future collisions

We can make the enemy disappear using the **hide** code block, and we've already seen how the script can be ended using **stop script**. The only thing left, then, is the score.

Create a new variable called `score`, and this time make sure that **For all sprites** is selected. This ensures that all sprites have access to the score, so if there are multiple enemies, they can all update the same variable. Once the variable has been created, make sure the box next to it is marked so the score appears on the Stage.

Now we need to add some code so the score increases when the enemy is hit. Add **change score by 10** inside the **forever if** block.

Your script should now look similar to the following screenshot:

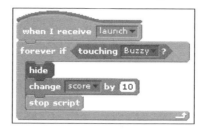

Test your game by playing it and trying to hit this enemy. Remember that you can adjust the sizes of the sprites, their launch speed, and the gravity, if the game is too hard or too easy. You will notice that once you hit the enemy, it disappears and you get points, but the score and enemies don't reset when you play again. Let's fix this. Add the code shown in the following screenshot to the enemy sprite as a second script:

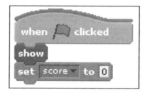

Now the enemy should come back, and the score should reset to 0 every time you click on the green flag.

Only when you've finished all the code should you create multiple enemies. Right-click on the enemy sprite in the Sprite list and click on **Duplicate** to create a copy. This copy will have all the necessary code with it to update the score and disappear after it has been hit. Create as many copies as you like, place them wherever you like, and then sit back and enjoy your game! It should look like the following screenshot:

# Extensions

So far we have created the bare minimum for a game. There are all sorts of extra features we could add, such as the following:

- Animation when two sprites collide
- A special enemy that gives bonus points
- Barriers that slow the player down
- Power-ups that increase the player's speed or flip gravity, for example
- Extra controls so the player can continue to affect the character after it has been launched

I will leave the rest of your game up to you, but here are some example scripts to give you some ideas. Try to work out what they do and where they might go, or just try them out! Some scripts may require minor modifications elsewhere to fit in properly.

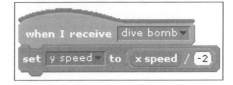

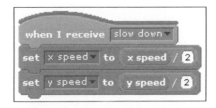

# Summary

In this chapter, we got to grips with the Scratch programming language. We learned that it can be easy to create animations, and we went as far as creating an entire game.

In the next chapter, we'll take our knowledge of Scratch and see how we can apply it to a different programming language called Python. There, we'll make another game and our own game controller to go with it.

# 3

# Testing Your Speed

In this chapter, we're going to create a new game that will test how quickly the player can react. To do this, we will create our own game controller—something you can't do on a normal computer—and write a program to handle when the controller's buttons are to be pressed.

If you do not have the components required to create the controller, an alternative program that uses the keyboard instead is provided at the end of the chapter. It is very similar to the default program, so it is still worth reading through this chapter to learn how everything works.

## Materials needed

The materials that are required to make your own controller are shown in the following figure. Think about what you would like your controller to look like and how many buttons it should have, as this will determine how many of each item you will need.

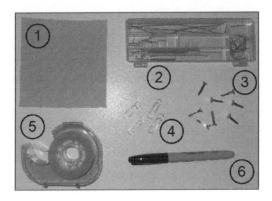

The previous figure shows the items we need to create a controller, and the details are as follows:

- Card (**1**) (as large as you want the controller to be)
- Wire (**2**)
- Paper fasteners (**3**) (2 x number of buttons)
- Paper clips (**4**) (1 x number of buttons; each clip should be plain metal with no coating)
- Sticky tape (**5**)
- Pens/pencils for decoration (**6**)

If you already have some electric switches you'd like to use, you will not need the paper fasteners, paper clips, or sticky tape, but I think it's more fun to make everything from scratch!

We also need a safe way of connecting the wires to the Raspberry Pi. One approach is to use special male-to-female wires, which behave like normal wires at one end, but can be connected to a pin or another wire at the other end. The other way is to use a Raspberry Pi breakout board, a ribbon cable, and a breadboard. These three work together to give a larger area for plugging in electronic components. *Adafruit* is a great online shop that sells these sorts of components for the Raspberry Pi; you even get explanations on how to use them (`http://www.adafruit.com/category/105`).

# Creating the game controller

In order to design a controller, we first need to know what sort of game is going to be played. I am going to explain how to make a game where the player is told a letter, and they have to press the button of that letter as quickly as possible. They then are told another letter. The player has to hit as many buttons correctly as they can in a 30 second time limit.

There are many ways in which this game can be varied; instead of ordering the player to press a particular button, the game could ask the player a multiple-choice question, and instead of colors, the buttons could be labeled with `Yes`, `No`, `Maybe` or different colors. You could give the player multiple commands at once, and make sure that they press all the buttons in the right order. It would even be possible to make a huge controller and treat it as more of a board game. I will leave the game design up to you, but I recommend that you follow the instructions in this chapter until the end, and then change things to your liking once you know how everything works.

# The controller base

So now that we know how the game is going to be played, it's time to design the controller. This is what my design looks like with four different letters:

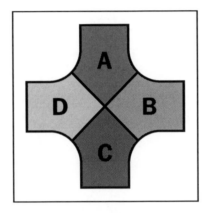

Make sure each button area is at least a little bigger than a paper clip, as these are what the buttons will be made of. I recommend a maximum of eight buttons.

Draw your design on to the card, decorate it however you like, and then cut it out.

# Adding buttons

Now for each button, we need to perform the following steps:

1. Poke two small holes in the card, roughly 3 cm apart (or however long your paper clips are), as shown in the following figure. Use a sharp pencil or a pair of scissors to do this.

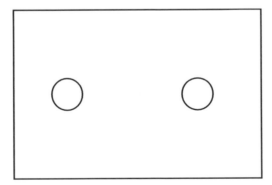

2. Push a paper fastener through each hole and open them out, as shown in the following figures:

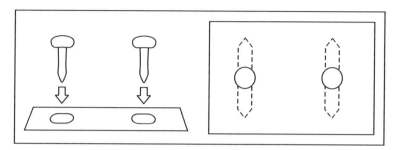

3. Wrap a paper clip around the head of one of the fasteners, and (if necessary) bend it so that it grips the fastener tightly, as shown in the following figure:

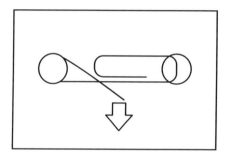

4. Bend the other end of the paper clip up very slightly, so it doesn't touch the second fastener unless you press down on it, as shown in the following figure:

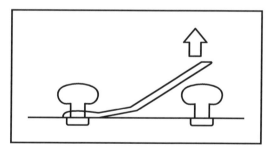

5.  Turn the card over and tape one leg of each fastener in place, making sure that they don't touch, as shown in the following figure:

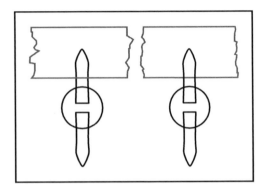

6.  Tape a length of wire to each of the two remaining legs of the fasteners. The ends of the wires should be exposed metal so that electricity can flow through the wire, paper fastener, and paper clip (as shown in the following figure). You may like to delay this step until later, when you have a better idea of how long the wire should be.

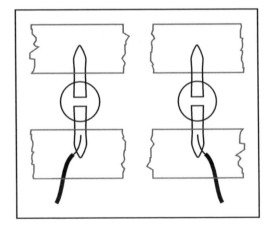

# Connecting to the Raspberry Pi

Now that the controller is ready, it's time to connect it to the Raspberry Pi. One of the things that distinguishes the Raspberry Pi from a normal computer is its set of **general purpose input/output (GPIO)** pins. These are the 26 pins at the top-left corner of the Raspberry Pi, just above the logo. As the name suggests, they can be used for any purpose, and are capable of both sending and receiving signals.

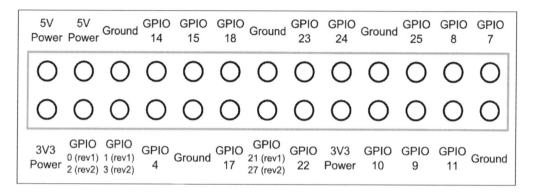

The preceding figure shows what each of the pins does. In order to create a (useful) circuit, we need to connect one of the power pins to one of the ground pins, with some sort of electrical component in between. The GPIO pins are particularly useful because we can make them behave like either power or ground pins, and they can also detect what they're connected to.

Note that there are two versions of the pin numbering system. You will almost certainly have a revision 2 Raspberry Pi. The revision 2 board has two mounting holes, while the revision 1 board has none. (These holes are surrounded by metal and are large enough to put a screw through. It's easy to spot them if they're there.) It is safest to simply not use any of the pins that have different numbers in different revisions.

To connect your controller to the Raspberry Pi, connect one wire from each button to a 3V3 power pin, and each of the remaining wires to a different GPIO pin (one with GPIO in its name as in the previous figure). In my example, I will use pins 22, 23, 24, and 25. Everything is now connected as shown in the following figure:

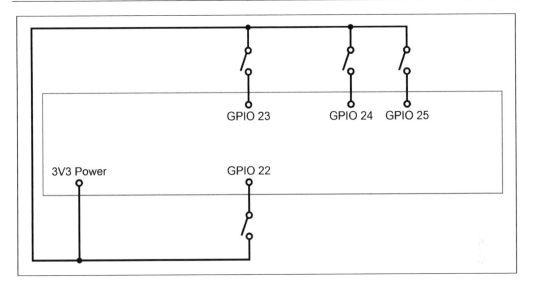

# Python

In this chapter, we are going to use the Python programming language. Almost all programming languages are capable of doing the same things, but they are usually designed with different specializations. Some languages are designed to perform one job particularly well, some are designed to run code as fast as possible, and some are designed to be easy to read.

Scratch was designed to make animations and games, and to be easy to read and learn, but it can be difficult to manage large programs. Python is designed to be a good all-round language. It is easy to read and can run code much faster than Scratch.

Python is a text-based language. We will type the code rather than arrange building blocks. This makes it easier to go back and change the pieces of code that we have already written, and it allows us to write complex pieces of code more quickly. Lots of tutorials and information about the available features are provided online at http://docs.python.org/2/. *Learn Python the Hard Way* is another good learning resource, which is available at http://learnpythonthehardway.org.

As an example, let's take a look at some Scratch code and some Python code which do the same thing, as shown in the following figure:

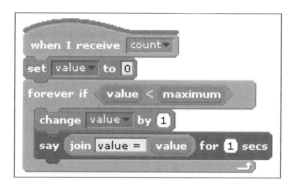

The Python code that does the same job looks like the following code snippet:

```
def count(maximum):
    value = 0
    while value < maximum:
        value = value + 1
        print "value =", value
```

Even if you've never seen any Python code before, you might be able to read it and tell what it does. Both pieces of code count from 0 to a maximum value, and display the value each time.

The biggest difference is on the first line. Instead of waiting for a message, we **define** (or create) a function, and instead of sending a message, we **call** the function. (More on how to run Python code shortly.) Notice that we include maximum as an **argument** to the count function. This tells Python the particular value we mean to be the maximum, and allows us to reuse the name maximum in different parts of the code—very useful when we have a lot of variables and need to name them all!

The other main differences are that we have while instead of forever if, and we have print instead of say. These are just different ways of writing the same thing. Also, instead of having a block of code wrap around other blocks, we simply put an extra four spaces at the beginning of a line to show which code is contained within a particular block.

To run a piece of Python code, open IDLE on the Raspberry Pi desktop. Type the previous code into IDLE and you should notice that it can recognize how many spaces to start a line with. When you have finished, press *Enter* a couple of times, until you see >>>. This shows that Python recognizes that your block of code has completed, and that it is ready to receive a new command. Now, you can run your code by typing in count (5) and pressing *Enter*. You can change the 5 to any number you like. We're now ready to create our game!

# Coding the game

Here's a quick recap on how this example game is going to work. The Raspberry Pi will choose a random button and ask the player to press it. Every time the player presses the right button, they get a point, and every time they press a wrong button, they lose a point. Once the right button has been pressed, the Raspberry Pi selects a new button as the target. The aim is to score as many points as possible in 30 seconds.

In IDLE, navigate to **File | New Window**. This will bring up a new empty window, which is where all our code will go. This window is better for editing existing code, and I will call it the **Edit window**. Whenever you want to test or run your code, navigate to **Run | Run Module**, or press *F5* on your keyboard. This will take you back to the first window, which I will call the **Shell**, with the code ready to run.

# Random behavior

The first job, then, is to write some code that will choose a random button for the player to press. Take a look at the following code snippet. There are a few new things here, so we'll go through them one by one afterwards.

```
import random
options = [22, 23, 24, 25]

def nexttarget():
    target = random.choice(options)
    print target
    return target
```

On the first line of the code, we import the random module. Python comes with a huge amount of code that other people have written for us, separated into different modules. Some of this code is simple, but makes life more convenient for us, and some of it is complex, allowing us to reuse other people's solutions to the challenges we face and concentrate on exactly what we want to do. In this case, we are making use of a collection of functions that deal with random behavior. We must import a module before we are able to access its contents. Information on the default modules available can be found online.

On the second line of the code, we create a list of options. These are the GPIO pins that the buttons are connected to, and we show that it is a list by surrounding it with square brackets.

Next, we create a function called `nexttarget`. The empty brackets afterwards show that we do not need to pass any information to this function for it to work. The function chooses one of the options at random and stores it in a variable called `target`. The name `random.choice` tells us that we are using a function called `choice`, which can be found inside the `random` module that we imported earlier. We then print the target to display it to the player, and return the target to whichever piece of code asked for it.

You can test your code now if you like. Type it all into the Edit window and run it. Type `nexttarget()` next to the `>>>` marker in the Shell and press *Enter*, and you should see numbers being displayed. You can do this as many times as you like to make sure random pins are being displayed. The problem is that if the player is told to press pin 22, he might not know which button that means. Let's change our code to improve that. Go back to the Edit window and update your code as follows:

```
import random
options = {22:"A", 23:"B", 24:"C", 25:"D"}

def nexttarget():
    target = random.choice(options.keys())
    print options[target]
    return target
```

The main difference is that we've changed `options` from a list to a dictionary. (Note the curly brackets instead of square ones.) Using a dictionary allows us to give each pin a name, which will be more useful to the player. In this case, I have connected pin 22 to the A button, and so on. In proper coding terms, the dictionary links each **key** (pin number) with a **value** (name). Our target pin must therefore be chosen from the dictionary's keys, so we add `.keys()` on the line where we choose a pin. Finally, when we display the target to the player, we get its name from the dictionary using the square brackets.

# Using the controller

Next, we need to detect which button is currently being pressed. Look at the following code snippet:

```
import RPi.GPIO as GPIO

def buttonpressed():
```

```
    for pin in options.keys():
        if GPIO.input(pin) == GPIO.HIGH:
            return pin
    else:
        return None
```

Once again, we're importing a module that does some of the behind-the-scenes work for us. This time, we've used as to give it a slightly shorter name, which will hopefully make the rest of the code easier to read. We usually put all imports together at the very top of the code, as this makes it easier to see them all at once. All the code for this chapter is shown together towards the end, if you are unsure where to put a particular piece of code.

Inside the buttonpressed function, we have a for loop. This is a bit like the forever if block in Scratch, except we tell it to stop after it has run a certain number of times. In this case, we tell it to run once for each of the pins in our dictionary of options.

We then check to see what signal that pin is receiving. If it is receiving GPIO.LOW, we know that the button is not being pressed, but if it is receiving GPIO.HIGH, we know that the button is being pressed and that there is a connection from this pin, through the button, to the power pin. (In electronics, we say a signal is *low* if it is connected to ground and *high* if it is connected to the voltage supply.) If the button is being pressed, we return the pin number. Look out for the double-equals sign here; a single-equals sign is used to give a variable a new value, but a double-equals sign checks to see if two values are the same. If none of the pins are being pressed, we return the special value None.

Before we can access the pins, we need to prepare them. Since they can be used for any purpose, we need to tell them what their job is for this particular piece of code. Add the following function to your code in the Edit window:

```
def preparepins():
    GPIO.setmode(GPIO.BCM)
    for pin in options.keys():
        GPIO.setup(pin, GPIO.IN, pull_up_down = GPIO.PUD_DOWN)
```

The GPIO.setmode line selects a particular numbering scheme for the Raspberry Pi's pins. Then, we have another for loop that looks at each of the pins in turn. For each pin, we choose GPIO.IN to say that it should be an input and receive signals, and we use GPIO.PUD_DOWN to say that if nothing is connected to the pin, its signal should be pulled down to behave like GPIO.LOW (no button press). This function will need to be run before we receive any signals from the pins in buttonpressed. (If you do try to run this code now, you may get some strange error messages. We'll address those soon.)

# Adding a time limit

We can make sure that `prepareprins` is always run before `buttonpressed` by writing it into our program. Let's now start building the function that brings everything together to create a game. For now, we want to set up the GPIO pins and make sure the game lasts the correct length of time.

```python
import time

def play(duration):
    prepareprins()

    start = time.time()
    end = start + duration

    while time.time() < end:
        # Do stuff
        time.sleep(0.1)
```

Once again, we are importing a module of the existing code to do some of the hard work for us. This time, it's a module full of functions that deal with time, and we are particularly interested in the one that tells us what the current time is.

Notice that we give `duration` as an argument to the `play` function. This lets us easily change the length of the game later, if we like. We then make absolutely sure that `prepareprins` happens first by executing it straight away.

Next, we make a note of the current time using `time.time()`, and store it in a variable called `start`. We calculate the time at which the game should end by adding the length of the game to the current time.

We then enter a `while` block (or `forever if`, if you prefer), which continues until the current time passes the time when the game should end. Inside the `while` block, we have a comment beginning with `#`. Comments are ignored by Python, but are useful for the programmer. You can leave notes for yourself, to explain what a piece of code does. In this case, we've left a comment to say that there is more code to go inside, but we'll come back to it later. Finally, we put our program to sleep for 0.1 seconds. This has the following two purposes:

- It ensures that we don't waste time checking whether the buttons are pressed immediately after a previous check.

- It makes reading from the pins more reliable. In the instant after pressing a button, the paper clip may actually bounce up and down a tiny bit, making it seem like the button is being pressed multiple times. The way this game works, the player could end up losing points as the game may think the wrong button is being pressed.

# Bringing it all together

Now, let's fill in the gaps and turn our program into a game. We want to use `nexttarget` and `buttonpressed` together to tell whether the right or wrong button is being pressed, and we want to keep track of the score. Update your `play` function so it looks like the following code snippet:

```
def play(duration):
    preparepins()

    start = time.time()
    end = start + duration
    score = 0

    target = nexttarget()
    while time.time() < end:
        button = buttonpressed()
        if button == target:
            score = score + 1
            print "Correct!"
            target = nexttarget()
        elif button != None:
            score = score - 1
            print "Wrong!"
        time.sleep(0.1)

    print "Your final score is", score
```

The following is what's changed:

- We've created a new variable called `score`, which starts at `0`. Whenever the player presses the right button, the score goes up, and whenever they press the wrong button, it goes down. At the end of the game, we display the final score.

- We added another new variable called `target`. This is the pin connected to the button that we want the player to press. We set a target using `nexttarget` when the game first starts, and we update the target whenever the player presses the correct button.

- Inside the `while` block, we check which button is being pressed (if any). If the pressed button is the same as the target button, we give the player a point. Otherwise, if a different button is being pressed, we take a point away. `elif` is short for `else if`, and is used when we have multiple `if` blocks, but only want one of them to be executed.

That's it! The game is ready to play. There's just one final small piece of code to add to the very end of the program, which could make things easier for us later:

```
if __name__ == "__main__":
    play(30)
```

This is a special small trick that allows us to reuse our code later as its own module, or just play the game without having to load and run all of the code in IDLE first.

Now, if you try to play the game, you will probably get an error message. This is because the Raspberry Pi's operating system wants to protect all of the hardware. You could end up doing dangerous things if you were allowed to change whatever you like! In this case, though, our actions are limited to the GPIO pins, so we can be fairly sure that we won't break anything. Save your code and close down IDLE. Open LXTerminal and type in `sudo idle <name of program>`. You might be asked to enter your password (the default is `raspberry`). You should see IDLE open up, and it should look exactly the same as before. This time, however, you should be able to navigate to **Run | Run Module** and type in `play(30)` to play the game. The difference is the `sudo` command. This tells the Raspberry Pi that we know what we're doing and that we're sure we're not going to damage anything.

Be very careful when using the `sudo` command because the computer will always do exactly what you tell it to do, even if this means causing permanent damage.

Our little extra piece of code at the end of the program gives us a different way of starting the game. Close down IDLE and type `sudo python <name of program>` into the terminal. The game should start much more quickly this time.

# Complete code listing

The complete code listing section shows the complete program. This may be useful if you're not sure where the different code snippets should go, or if your program isn't working and you want to compare it to something that works.

```
import RPi.GPIO as GPIO
import random
import time

options = {22:"A", 23:"B",
```

```
4:"C", 25:"D"}

def preparepins():
    GPIO.setmode(GPIO.BCM)
    for pin in options.keys():
        GPIO.setup(pin, GPIO.IN, pull_up_down = GPIO.PUD_DOWN)

def nexttarget():
    target = random.choice(options.keys())
    print options[target]
    return target


def buttonpressed():
    for pin in options.keys():
        if GPIO.input(pin) == GPIO.HIGH:
            return pin
    else:
        return None

def play(duration):
    preparepins()

    start = time.time()
    end = start + duration
    score = 0

    target = nexttarget()
    while time.time() < end:
        button = buttonpressed()
        if button == target:
            score = score + 1
            print "Correct!"
            target = nexttarget()
        elif button != None:
            score = score - 1
            print "Wrong!"
        time.sleep(0.1)

    print "Your final score is", score

if __name__ == "__main__":
  play(30)
```

# The keyboard version

If you do not have access to the components necessary to create your own controller, here is a slightly modified program that uses the keyboard instead. You might notice that its structure is exactly the same as the previous program. Separating tasks out into different functions allows us to make changes like these quickly and easily.

```python
import pygame, pygame.event, pygame.key
from pygame.locals import *
import random
import time

options = {K_UP:"up", K_DOWN:"down", K_LEFT:"left", K_RIGHT:"right"}

def prepare():
    pygame.init()
    screen = pygame.display.set_mode((250, 1))
    pygame.display.set_caption("Test your speed!")

def nexttarget():
    target = random.choice(options.keys())
    print options[target]
    return target


def keypressed():
    pygame.event.pump()
    keyspressed = pygame.key.get_pressed()
    for key in options.keys():
        if keyspressed[key]:
            return key
    else:
        return None

def play(duration):
    prepare()

    start = time.time()
    end = start + duration
    score = 0

    target = nexttarget()
    while time.time() < end:
        key = keypressed()          if key == target:
            score = score + 1
            print "Correct!"
```

```
        target = nexttarget()
    elif key != None:
        score = score - 1
        print "Wrong!"
    time.sleep(0.1)

print "Your final score is", score

pygame.quit()

if __name__ == "__main__":
    play(30)
```

# What's next?

Now that your game is working, you might like to try using most of the same code to create different games. (I suggest that if you make changes, you save it to a different file, so you don't lose your current game.) In particular, you could change `nexttarget()` so that it asks a question and gives some possible answers, and the player has to choose an answer as quickly as possible. Alternatively, you could create a Simon Says style game, where the game gives a sequence of buttons that must be pressed, and the player tries to repeat it.

If you have an Internet connection and are feeling adventurous, you could try using your controller to play your Angry Birds game from the previous chapter. Search the Internet for *ScratchGPIO* to download an enhanced version of Scratch, and try to explore how it can interact with the Raspberry Pi's GPIO pins.

If you're interested in learning more about electronics and what you can do with GPIO, take a look at Adafruit's online tutorials at `http://learn.adafruit.com/category/learn-raspberry-pi`.

# Summary

In this chapter, we used the Python programming language to create a game. We created an electronic circuit to act as the game controller, and used code to detect when the buttons were being pressed. We learned the basics of the Python language, and saw how separating the code into multiple functions makes it more flexible and easier to manage.

In the next chapter, we will build on this Python knowledge to create an interactive map.

# 4

# Making an Interactive Map of Your City

In this chapter, we're going to learn more about Python and its available modules by creating a program that will allow us to create notes on a map of our local area.

A program such as this needs a proper **graphical user interface (GUI)**, which is just a complicated way of saying that it is a visual program, with things to see and buttons to click. Here's what the program looks like when it's finished:

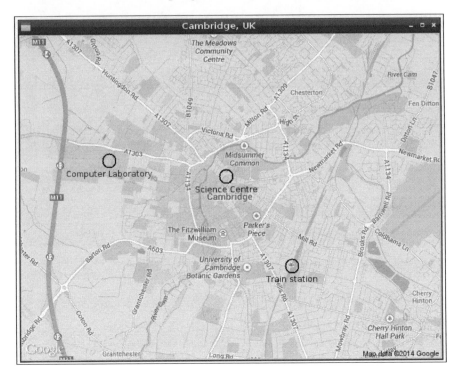

As you can see, the program looks quite professional with its title bar and buttons. You will be able to click on locations on the map and give helpful labels. By the end of the chapter, you will know enough about building GUIs to be able to add all sorts of additional features.

# Hello world!

As is traditional when we learn about a new technology, we're going to start with the simplest program possible, just to make sure that we understand the basics. In this case, we're going to create a basic window with a title and some text inside.

# Tkinter

There are many different Python modules available that let us create graphical programs, but we're going to use one called Tkinter. This module is included with Python by default and works on almost all computers and operating systems.

Tkinter has easy-to-use functions to create textboxes, buttons, scroll bars, menus, and more. Collectively, these components are called **widgets**. To create a graphical user interface, we combine a number of widgets with a **layout**, which tells Tkinter how the widgets should be arranged. For example, we could say that all of the buttons should be in a row or that they should be arranged vertically.

There is a summary of how to use the available widgets in the *Extensions* section at the end of this chapter.

# Writing the program

Before we start, open a fresh IDLE window and make sure you are at the Edit window (navigate to **File | New Window**). The first thing we want to do is to import the `Tkinter` module so we can make use of all the functions it contains; therefore, add the following line of code at the top of the file:

```
import Tkinter
```

Now would also be a good time to save the program and give it a useful name. Navigate to **File | Save** and save the program as `hellogui.py`.

Creating a window is very simple. All we need is the following code snippet:

```
window = Tkinter.Tk()
window.mainloop()
```

Leave a blank line below the import line (for neatness) and type in the preceding code. That's it! We can now run the program (either with **Run | Run Module** or by pressing *F5*), and we will see an empty window appear. The first line of code creates a window, and the second line of code tells it to enter its main loop. The main loop causes the window to be shown on the screen and lets it wait for any of its buttons to be pressed. (This is similar to how we had a loop in the previous chapter to wait for our controller buttons to be pressed.)

There are a couple more very simple things we can do before we move on to creating the main program. This extra code must go between the previous two lines. The final `mainloop` line doesn't finish until the window is closed, so any code that comes afterwards will run too late to be shown on the screen. First, we can give the window a title as follows:

```
window.title("Some text here")
```

We can give the window any title we like. Secondly, we're going to place a simple widget in the window that displays some text as follows:

```
label = Tkinter.Label(window, text="Hello!")
label.pack()
```

This code is a little more complex. First, we create a Label widget—a widget for displaying text (or images). When we're creating it, we pass in two arguments: the window we've created and the text to be shown. Note that the second one has the name `text`, but the first one doesn't have a name at all. In Python, functions can have the option of receiving lots of different arguments. All of the essential ones come first and don't need names; we can tell them apart from the order they are in. After that come the optional arguments. We need to give names to these so the function can tell which arguments have been left out. We need the first argument because the Label widget needs to know which window it will be in. In more advanced GUIs, we can even tell widgets which sections of the GUI they should go in. The second line of code packs the Label widget to work out what size it is and start displaying it.

You might notice if you run your program now that the window has shrunk to fit the Label widget we just added, so we can't see the title anymore! We can fix this by telling the window the minimum size it is allowed to be as shown in the following code snippet:

```
width = 200
height = 50
window.minsize(width, height)
```

You might like to tweak the width if you have a long window title. You should now have a window that looks similar to the following screen:

Now that the window has a minimum size, you will notice that if you drag the edges of the window, you can make it larger; however, you can't make it any smaller.

We're now ready to move on. The following is a complete code for this simple example. I've grouped some of the lines together to keep things organized, but the main point is that anything involving the way the window looks happens between the window being created and the window's main loop starting, as shown in the following code snippet:

```
import Tkinter
width = 200
height = 50
window = Tkinter.Tk()
window.title("Some text here")
window.minsize(width, height)
label = Tkinter.Label(window, text="Hello!")
label.pack()
window.mainloop()
```

# Getting a map

In this section, we're going to use Google Maps to get an image of our local area to display it in our window.

# No Internet? No problem!

Since Google Maps is an online service, an Internet connection is required to download a map. However, if your Raspberry Pi isn't connected to the Internet, there is still a way to proceed. Python is cross-platform. This means that it works on lots of different computers and operating systems. So long as you have access to another computer that does have an Internet connection, all of the code in this chapter will work.

Python can be downloaded from `http://www.python.org/download/`, and the code in this book is based on Python 2.7. (Python is often preinstalled on Linux operating systems, and it is best to keep it up to date with your built-in packaging system.) Once installed on any computer, IDLE will be available and should behave exactly as it does on the Raspberry Pi.

# Google Maps

Google has made it very easy to access its maps from programs that we've written ourselves (up to a 1000 times per day). All we need to do is create a web address with all the information about the map we want.

All addresses start with `https://maps.googleapis.com/maps/api/staticmap?` and contain all sorts of information, separated by & symbols after the question mark:

- `center=location`: This is some text describing where the location that the map should show. It could be a town name, or a postal code, or the name of a road or building. Web addresses should not contain any spaces, so if your chosen location does have spaces, they should be replaced by the + symbol.

- `zoom=value`: This is a number that increases as we zoom in to the map. Around 13 to 14 seems to give good results for this project, but you might like to try other values.

- `size=widthxheight`: These are values in pixels. In this chapter, I'm going to use a width of 640 pixels and a height of 480 pixels.

- `format=type` (optional): This denotes the format of the image to be downloaded, such as .jpeg, .gif, and .png (default). In this chapter, we're going to use .gif as it works best with Tkinter.

- `maptype=type` (optional): This tells us what view of the map we should get. Do we want a satellite image or a roadmap, or do we want to see the terrain? If we don't choose a map type, we will get a road map.

- `sensor=true/false`: This tells us if we are using GPS (or something similar) to choose the location. For this project, it will always be set to false.

A full list of available options and their explanations can be found online at `https://developers.google.com/maps/documentation/staticmaps/#URL_Parameters`.

So, an example web address might be `https://maps.googleapis.com/maps/api/staticmap?center=Cambridge,%20UK&zoom=13&size=640x480&format=gif&sensor=false`. Here, I have chosen the map of Cambridge, UK, with a zoom level of 13, and an image that is 640 x 480 pixels and in the .gif format. You may want to type this address into a web browser and play with the various options to see what's possible.

# Generating the address

So, how do we create these long web addresses automatically in our program? It turns out that Python makes this very easy for us with its `format` function. The `format` function takes some text and looks through it for markers that look like {0}, where 0 can be any number. Whenever it sees one of these markers, it replaces it with its argument at that position as shown in the following code snippet:

```
"{0}".format(14) gives "14"
"Second = {1}, first = {0}".format(1, 2) gives "Second = 2,
first = 1"
```

The main thing to look out for is that programming languages like to start counting from zero, so if you want to access the first argument of the format, you use {0}, and if you want the seventh argument, you use {6}.

To generate our address, we can use the following code snippet:

```
address = "http://maps.googleapis.com/maps/api/staticmap?\
center={0}&zoom={1}&size={2}x{3}&format=gif&sensor=false"\
.format(location, zoom, width, height)
```

This is just a slightly longer and more complex version of what we've seen already. The \ symbols allow us to break the line into multiple parts so it doesn't go off the edge of the screen (or page), and they do not show up in the final address if we start a new line immediately after the \ symbol.

To make our code more readable and useful, it is best if we put this address creation code in a separate function. This way, we can generate addresses any time we like when the program is running, without having to copy the code.

Place the following code snippet immediately after the `import` statement in `hellogui.py`, and then save it to a new file called `mapping.py`:

```
import urllib
def getaddress(location, width, height, zoom):
    locationnospaces = urllib.quote_plus(location)
    address = "http://maps.googleapis.com/maps/api/staticmap?\
center={0}&zoom={1}&size={2}x{3}&format=gif&sensor=false"\
.format(locationnospaces, zoom, width, height)
    return address
```

You'll notice that there's an extra line at the start of the function that uses `urllib.quote_plus` to make sure that there are no spaces in the name of the location by replacing them with + symbols. It can also handle any other characters that aren't allowed in web addresses. We had to import the `urllib` module first to get access to this function. The `urllib` module is short for URL library and allows us to access information over the Internet. **Uniform Resource Locator (URL)** is just another name for a web address. You may want to provide extra options to add extra arguments to the function later.

We can now see if our code works. Run the program and close the window that pops up—we're not interested in it for the moment. In the Shell (next to the >>> marker), type in `getaddress("Cambridge, UK", 640, 480, 13)`, press *Enter*, and check that the link is the same as the example earlier. You can even paste it into a web browser to check that it works.

If you're really keen on controlling things with code, try out the following code snippet:

```
import webbrowser
webbrowser.open(getaddress("Cambridge, UK", 640, 480, 13))
```

# Downloading the image

Now that we can create a web address for our map, we want to download it for use in our program. To do this, we're going to create another function called `getmap` that uses `getaddress`. The `getmap` function must therefore come after `getaddress` in our program but still before the part at the end where we create the window. Here's the code snippet:

```
import base64
def getmap(location, width, height, zoom):
    address = getaddress(location, width, height, zoom)
    urlreader = urllib.urlopen(address)
    data = urlreader.read()
    urlreader.close()
    base64data = base64.encodestring(data)
    image = Tkinter.PhotoImage(data=base64data)
    return image
```

We first need to import another module. The `base64` module allows us to convert the downloaded image data into something that Tkinter can use.

The first thing we do in our new function is create an address using the previous function. We can then connect to this address using `urllib.urlopen` and download the data using `read`. We make sure to tidy up afterwards by using `close`. The `urlreader` object might have used some temporary storage that is no longer needed now that we have the data.

Unfortunately, the data we downloaded isn't in a form that Tkinter can use, so we need to convert it using `base64.encodestring`. You don't need to understand how this works; just be aware that it's there. (If you're interested in what's going on inside the module, take a look at `http://docs.python.org/2/library/base64.html`.) Finally, we convert the data into an image using `Tkinter.PhotoImage` and return it.

# Using the image

We now have an image ready to use, so it's time to display it in our program. It is possible to put the image inside the Label widget that we already have, but we will want to draw on top of it later, so we will use a Canvas widget instead. You can think of a Canvas widget as a bit like the canvas an artist would use. It allows us to draw all sorts of shapes and text in any color we like. For now, we're just going to draw our map.

Replace the two lines of code that mention the Label widget with the following code snippet:

```
mapimage = getmap(location, width, height, zoom)
canvas = Tkinter.Canvas(window, width=width, height=height)
canvas.create_image(0,0,image=mapimage,anchor=Tkinter.NW)
canvas.pack()
```

First, we get the image using our `getmap` function. We then create a Canvas inside our window with a particular width and height. Then, we draw our image on the Canvas. We say that we want the northwest (NW) corner of the image to be placed at coordinates `(0,0)` within the Canvas. Since the northwest and coordinates `(0,0)` both mean the top-left corner, and the Canvas is the same size as the image, the image will fill the Canvas exactly. Finally, we `pack` the Canvas widget as we did with the Label widget.

One last thing to do is give some sensible values for `location`, `width`, `height`, and `zoom`. We already have values for the width and height, but we'd like our map to be a little larger than our previous window. Replace the old `width =` and `height =` lines with the following code snippet:

```
location = "Cambridge, UK"
width = 640
height = 480
zoom = 13
```

Feel free to experiment with different values. When you run your program, you should now see something like the following screenshot:

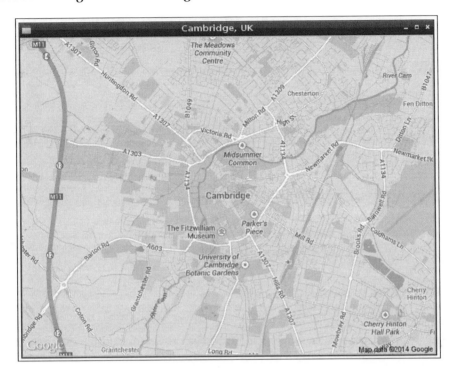

I have also updated the title of the window to use `location` rather than `"Some text here"` from before. If your code isn't working, it's likely that there's either a spelling mistake somewhere, some code needs to be moved up or down within the program, or Python isn't sure which blocks of code are meant to be inside which other blocks. Remember that the number of spaces at the beginning of each line is very important. The recommendation is to use four spaces for each level of indentation. For example, the very first line of a function (in this project) should have no spaces in front of it, code inside that function should have four spaces at the start of each line, and code inside an `if` or `while` block inside that function should be indented with another four spaces. If you're stuck, take a look at the code listing near the end of the chapter.

# Adding markers

The next thing we want to do is add a marker to the map whenever we click on it with the mouse. This can be done in two parts: by detecting the click and reacting to the click.

# Detecting mouse clicks

Detecting mouse clicks is very simple. Tkinter does most of the work for us. All we have to do is **bind** a function to the mouse button. Once the program has entered its main loop, whenever the mouse button creates an event (by being clicked), the function will be executed. Reacting to an event in this way is similar to using a `when key pressed` code block in Scratch. Place the following line of code with the rest of the Canvas code before the main loop:

```
canvas.bind("<Button-1>", canvasclick)
```

The preceding line of code says that whenever `Button-1` (the left mouse button) is clicked, run the `canvasclick` function. We'll write that function next.

We can create these bindings for as many buttons and keys as we like and for any widget that we like. The `"<Button-3>"` button is the right mouse button, `"<space>"` is the Space bar, `"<Return>"` is the *Enter* key, and `"a"`, `"b"`, `"c"`, and so on correspond to the letters. There are even events called `"<Enter>"` and `"<Leave>"` that can tell when the mouse moves over the widget.

# Reacting to mouse clicks

When the mouse button is clicked, an event is given to our `canvasclick` function. The event contains lots of information, including the position of the click, the widget that was clicked, and the key that was pressed (if any).

Here's a quick version of `canvasclick` that should let you make sure that mouse clicks are being detected properly. Place it beneath the `getmap` function as follows:

```
def canvasclick(event):
    print "Mouse click at position", event.x, event.y
```

When we run the program, we should now see pairs of numbers being displayed in the Shell whenever we click on our map. These numbers should change depending on where we click on the map. What we really want, though, is to draw a marker on the map so we can highlight interesting points. We'll replace the `print` line with the following code, and a circle will be drawn on the map at each position clicked:

```
x,y = event.x, event.y
widget = event.widget
size = 10
widget.create_oval(x-size, y-size, x+size, y+size, width=2)
```

We're going to use `event.x` and `event.y` a few times, so here we've given them the more convenient names of `x` and `y`. We've done the same thing for `event.widget` (the widget that received this mouse click event), giving it the more convenient name of `widget`. The `size` variable stores the distance, in pixels, from the click position to the edge of the circle. You can change it if you like.

Finally, we draw the circle using `widget.create_oval`. The first four arguments are the coordinates of the left, top, right, and bottom edges of the circle, and `width` is the width of the line used to draw the circle. You can add extra arguments such as `outline="red"` to change the color of the line and `fill="blue"` to change the internal color. I particularly like the `activeoutline` and `activefill` arguments, which work in the same way but only show their colors if the mouse is over the marker. Experiment until you have a marker design you like.

You should now have a program that looks like something similar to the following screenshot:

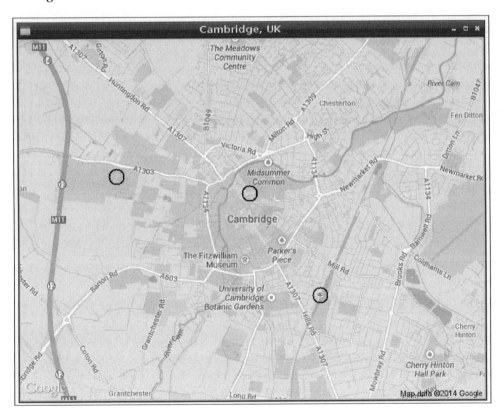

# Adding labels

It would be useful if whenever we clicked on the map, along with adding a circular marker, we could also add a few words to describe what it is we're marking.

## Basic labels

Getting some text from the program's user is going to be slightly complex, so let's create a simple version first to make sure we have the right code structure. Add the following two lines of code right at the end inside the `canvasclick` function:

```
label = getlabelname()
widget.create_text(x, y+2*size, text=label)
```

The first line of code gets some text from a function that we haven't written yet called `getlabelname`. This function will eventually ask the user to type some text into a small pop-up window, but for now, it will just give us a default message. The second line of code draws our text at a particular position just underneath the circle. As with `widget.create_oval` earlier, `widget.create_text` allows the text color to be set using the extra arguments of `fill="colour"` and `activefill="colour"`.

Here is our most basic version of the `getlabelname` function. We will flesh it out in the next section. Since it is used in `canvasclick`, `getlabelname` needs to be placed somewhere before it in the program. Putting `getlabelname` immediately above `canvasclick` is a good idea because the two functions are used together, and this way, we can see both of them in the Edit window at the same time as follows:

```
def getlabelname():
    text = "This is a label"
    return text
```

When you run your program, you should now see small text labels appear below the markers whenever you click on the map.

## Pop-up windows

Let's now make `getlabelname` a little more interesting. We're going to open a new window that asks the user to give a name for their marker. This window should have an instruction for the user telling them what to do, a place for the user to type their marker's name, and a button to click when they're finished.

First, we'll create a new window in a way similar to how we made our main window. Add the following code at the beginning of `getlabelname`, somewhere before the `return` line (there's a complete copy of the function at the end of this section if you're not sure where a particular piece of code should go):

```
popup = Tkinter.Tk()
popup.title("New marker")
popup.wait_window()
```

This time, we're using `Tkinter.Toplevel` instead of `Tkinter.Tk`. We only use `Tk` for the main window, and use `Toplevel` for all the others. The `wait_window()` method then behaves like `mainloop()`, and waits until the window is closed.

Next, we'll add a label with the instruction for the user. Remember that all the contents of a window must be created after the window is created but before we start its main loop. Type the following lines of code immediately above `popup.mainloop()`:

```
label = Tkinter.Label(popup, text="Please enter a label for your
marker")
label.pack()
```

The code so far is very similar to the very first window we created at the beginning of the chapter. You might like to try running the program and make sure that the new window does appear whenever you click on the map, and that the default label appears.

Next, we're going to add a textbox for the user to type into, as follows:

```
labelname = Tkinter.StringVar()
textbox = Tkinter.Entry(popup, textvariable=labelname)
textbox.pack()
textbox.focus_force()
```

There are a couple of new things here. First, we create a **StringVar** called `labelname`. StringVar is short for *String Variable*, and *string* is another word that programmers use for *text*. So, `labelname` is going to hold a text variable for us. Second, Tkinter's name for a textbox is **Entry**. This reflects the fact that we can enter text into the box, rather than simply viewing text which is already there. We pass our variable to the **Entry** when it is created. Now, we can access the text in the Entry through our variable—we'll get to this soon. As usual, we `pack` the **Entry** to prepare it to be displayed. Finally, we use `focus_force` to make sure that the textbox is the thing that has the user's attention. The pop-up window will now be the active window, and the textbox will be ready to type into. Without this line of code, the user would have to click on the textbox themselves before they could type anything in.

Next, we're going to add a button. When the button is clicked, the pop-up window should close, and we'll be ready to get the message out of the textbox. Here's the code we need:

```
button = Tkinter.Button(popup, text="Done")
button.pack()
```

This simply creates a new button that says **Done** in our new window. With this in place, the pop-up window should look finished. If you test your code now, you should see something like the following screenshot:

However, you'll notice that the button doesn't actually do anything yet. We need to give it a **command**. Update the button creation line as follows:

```
button = Tkinter.Button(popup, text="Done", command=popup.destroy)
```

Our window called `popup` has a function called `destroy` which closes the window. When the button is clicked, we want this function to be executed, so the window closes and we can retrieve the label name that the user typed in. To do this, we pass in the function as an extra argument when we create the button. Finally, to get the label name, replace the existing `text =` line with the following line of code:

```
text = labelname.get()
```

That's it! You should now be able to click on the map, type in a label name, and see it appears when you click on **Done**. Your running program should now look something like the following screenshot:

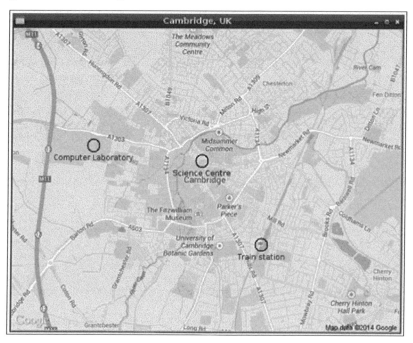

This is what your completed `getlabelname` function should look like:

```
def getlabelname():
    popup = Tkinter.Toplevel()
    popup.title("New marker")
    label = Tkinter.Label(popup, text="Please enter a label for your
marker")
    label.pack()

    labelname = Tkinter.StringVar()
    textbox = Tkinter.Entry(popup, textvariable=labelname)
    textbox.pack()
    textbox.focus_force()

    button = Tkinter.Button(popup, text="Done", command=popup.destroy)
    button.pack()

    popup.wait_window()

    text = labelname.get()
    return text
```

# Code listing

Here is the complete code for the project in this chapter. It can be used if you're getting strange error messages and want to compare your code with something that is known to work. It can also help you see which order the various snippets of code should be in.

The very first thing in the file should be the `import` statements. It's a good idea to put these in alphabetical order so we can search through them more quickly when we import a lot of modules; this is shown in the following code snippet:

```
import base64
import Tkinter

import urllib
```

Next, we have two functions that work together. The first one creates a web address and the second downloads the map image from that address as shown in the following code snippet:

```
def getaddress(location, width, height, zoom):
    locationnospaces = urllib.quote_plus(location)
    address = "http://maps.googleapis.com/maps/api/staticmap?\
center={0}&zoom={1}&size={2}x{3}&format=gif&sensor=false"\
.format(locationnospaces, zoom, width, height)
    return address
```

```
def getmap(location, width, height, zoom):
    address = getaddress(location, width, height, zoom)
    urlreader = urllib.urlopen(address)
    data = urlreader.read()
    urlreader.close()
    base64data = base64.encodestring(data)
    image = Tkinter.PhotoImage(data=base64data)
    return image
```

Then, we have the functions to deal with the pop-up window that collects the label to give to a marker on the map. The first function tells the window what to do when **Done** is clicked and the second then uses this function when it builds the window as shown in the following code snippet:

```
def getlabelname():
    popup = Tkinter.Toplevel()
    popup.title("New marker")
    label = Tkinter.Label(popup, text="Please enter a label for your
marker")
    label.pack()

    labelname = Tkinter.StringVar()
    textbox = Tkinter.Entry(popup, textvariable=labelname)
    textbox.pack()
    textbox.focus_force()

    button = Tkinter.Button(popup, text="Done", command=popup.destroy)
    button.pack()

    popup.wait_window()

    text = labelname.get()
    return text
```

We then have the function that is executed whenever the map is clicked. This makes use of the preceding functions as follows.

```
def canvasclick(event):
    x,y = event.x, event.y
    widget = event.widget
    size = 10
    widget.create_oval(x-size, y-size, x+size, y+size, width=2)
```

```
label = getlabelname()
widget.create_text(x, y+2*size, text=label)
```

Finally, we have the following code that has to be executed when we first run the program (this function is traditionally called `main`):

```
def main():
    location = "Cambridge, UK"
    width = 640
    height = 480
    zoom = 13

    window = Tkinter.Tk()
    window.title(location)
    window.minsize(width, height)

    mapimage = getmap(location, width, height, zoom)
    canvas = Tkinter.Canvas(window, width=width, height=height)
    canvas.create_image(0,0,image=mapimage,anchor=Tkinter.NW)
    canvas.bind("<Button-1>", canvasclick)
    canvas.pack()

    window.mainloop()

if __name__ == "__main__":
    main()
```

# Extensions

There are lots of things we could do now that we have a basic working GUI. Here are a few possible ideas:

- Add buttons to zoom in or out
- Add a textbox and button to update the location
- Add a way of selecting different styles of map marker
- Select whether the map is a satellite image or a road map
- Save and load the map settings (the location, position of markers, labels, and so on)
- Allow markers and their labels to be changed after they have been created

Complete details on how to use Tkinter can be found online at `https://wiki.python.org/moin/TkInter`.

# Layout

In this chapter, we have used only the `pack` layout, but there are also other ways of telling Python where you want your widgets to be displayed.

The `pack` layout is useful for filling the screen with a single widget (like our map) or placing widgets in a line (like our window for typing in label names).

The `grid` layout allows us to line up widgets both vertically and horizontally. All widgets that we put in the same column form a vertical line, and all widgets in the same row form a horizontal line. If no row or column is given, Python will put the widget in the first available place it finds. We can also have a widget reach across (or span) multiple rows or columns. Try replacing the three `.pack()` lines in `getlabelname` with the following lines of code:

```
label.grid(columnspan=2)
textbox.grid(column=0, row=1)
button.grid(column=1, row=1)
```

 The `pack` and `grid` layouts do not work together. If you would like to use one of these layouts, you will need to make sure that the same layout is used for every widget.

There is also a third option, `place`, which allows us to set the exact position of the widget. This isn't used often because `pack` and `grid` do such a good job, and it has too many necessary arguments to summarize here.

# Additional widgets

The next few sections give some very short code snippets showing how widgets that we haven't covered in this chapter can be created. If you want to test them out, put the code just before the `window.mainloop()` line in your program. The new widget will usually appear just below the map when you run the program. If you run out of space on your screen, try reducing the height of the map to make more space.

# Checkbutton

`Checkbutton` can either be empty or contain a check (tick).

```
state = Tkinter.StringVar()
checkbutton = Tkinter.Checkbutton(window, text="Button",
    variable=state, onvalue="checked", offvalue="unchecked")
checkbutton.pack()
```

Along with the button, we also need a `StringVar` variable (which is a text variable). The button has a particular value when it is on (`onvalue`) and a particular value when it is off (`offvalue`). These values are stored in the `StringVar` variable. To access the current state of the button, use `state.get()`.

# Frame and LabelFrame

Frames and LabelFrames simply contain other widgets. They allow us to structure lots of widgets better. A `Frame` is a plain container and a `LabelFrame` adds an outline and a label, as shown in the following code snippet:

```
labelframe = Tkinter.LabelFrame(window, text="LabelFrame")
button = Tkinter.Button(labelframe, text="Button")
button.pack()
labelframe.pack()
```

As you can see, we add `Button` to `LabelFrame` in the same way we would add it to a window, by passing `LabelFrame` as the first argument when we create the button.

# Listbox

`Listbox` has a different option on each line. Options can be selected and deselected by being clicked on. Let's have a look at the following code snippet:

```
options = Tkinter.StringVar()
options.set("Option1 Option2 Option3")
listbox = Tkinter.Listbox(window, listvariable=options)
listbox.pack()
```

Along with `Listbox`, we also need a `StringVar` variable to hold the available options. Each option is separated by a space. We can access the number of the current selection using `listbox.curselection()`. (Remember that programmers like to count from 0, so the first option is at position `0`.)

# Menu

`Menu` contains several different options, and some kind of action is taken when an option is clicked.

```
topmenu = Tkinter.Menu(window)
dropmenu = Tkinter.Menu(topmenu)
window["menu"] = topmenu
topmenu.add_cascade(label="Menu", menu=dropmenu)
dropmenu.add_command(label="Option1", command=function1)
dropmenu.add_command(label="Option2", command=function2)
```

Here, we are creating two menus. The first (topmenu) goes across the top of the screen. The second (dropmenu) drops down when it is clicked. The topmenu can contain any number of drop-down menus; these are added using topmenu.add_cascade. The dropmenu can contain any number of options; these are added using dropmenu. add_command. A different function is executed when each of the options is clicked. (I've just used the names function1 and function2 as examples. You will need to actually name the functions in your program.)

# Menubutton

Menubutton is very similar to dropdownmenu from the previous section, except that it is positioned as a button instead of within another menu at the top of the window. Let's take a look at the following code snippet:

```
menubutton = Tkinter.Menubutton(text="MenuButton")
menu = Tkinter.Menu(menubutton)
menubutton["menu"] = menu
menu.add_command(label="Option1", command=function1)
menu.add_command(label="Option2", command=function2)
menubutton.pack()
```

# Message

Message is a lot like Label, which we have already seen, except that it is designed for longer pieces of text and can spread across multiple lines as shown in the following code snippet:

```
message = Tkinter.Message(window, text="This is a message")
message.pack()
```

# OptionMenu

OptionMenu gives a drop-down list, allowing the user to select one of a fixed number of options, as shown in the following code snippet:

```
state = Tkinter.StringVar()
optionmenu = Tkinter.OptionMenu(window, state, "Option1",\
                                            "Option2")
optionmenu.pack()
```

We need a StringVar variable to hold the current selection, and this selection can be accessed using state.get().

# Radiobutton

Radiobuttons are usually used in groups, and only one can be selected at a time as shown in the following code snippet:

```
state = Tkinter.IntVar()
radiobutton1 = Tkinter.Radiobutton(window, text="Option1",\
                              value=1, variable=state)
radiobutton2 = Tkinter.Radiobutton(window, text="Option2",\
                              value=2, variable=state)
radiobutton1.pack()
radiobutton2.pack()
```

We need a variable to hold the current selection. This time we're using an `IntVar` variable (integer, which is a whole number variable), and each button has a value that will be stored in the variable when that button is selected. The key to only having one radio button selected at a time is to give the whole group the same variable argument. The current selection can be accessed using `state.get()`.

# Scale

`Scale` gives a slider that can be used to choose a value between two limits as shown in the following code snippet:

```
state = Tkinter.IntVar()
scale = Tkinter.Scale(window, label="Scale", from_=0, to=10,\
                   variable=state)
scale.pack()
```

We need `IntVar` (a whole number variable) to hold the current value, and we can choose the smallest and largest possible values using the `from_` and `to` arguments. We can get the current value of `Scale` using `state.get()`.

# Spinbox

`Spinbox` is a box containing a number. Next to the box are two small arrow buttons that make the number larger or smaller as shown in the following code snippet:

```
spinbox = Tkinter.Spinbox(window, from_=0, to=100, increment=10)
spinbox.pack()
```

We choose the smallest and largest possible values for `Spinbox` using the `from_` and `to` arguments, and we choose how much the value should change by when a button is pressed using increment. We can get the current value using `spinbox.get()`.

# Summary

In this chapter, we learned how to make a GUI in Python. We learned how to create all sorts of different widgets that let the GUI do interesting things, and we also learned how to react to events, such as mouse buttons, being clicked.

In particular, we created a mapping program that lets us click on the map to mark points of interest and even add useful descriptions for the markers. We have the knowledge and skills to add many extra features to our program by continuing to add buttons and other widgets.

Throughout this book, we've learned about the Raspberry Pi and what it can be used for. We've learned some core programming concepts and seen how they apply to both Scratch and Python. They apply to many other programming languages too. We've seen how programming can be a creative skill and can be used to create games or build useful tools. Above all, I hope you've found programming fun. It's a really valuable skill to learn and can provide unlimited entertainment.

If you've enjoyed this book and would like to continue your Raspberry Pi exploration, here are a few related books from *Packt Publishing* that you might find interesting:

- *Scratch 1.4: Beginner's Guide*
- *Raspberry Pi Cookbook for Python Programmers*
- *Instant Minecraft: Pi Edition Coding How-to*
- *Raspberry Pi for Secret Agents*

# Index

## Symbols

&lt;program name&gt; [extra information] command 14

## A

**Adafruit**
  URL 38, 53
**additional widgets**
  Checkbutton 72, 73
  Frame 73
  LabelFrame 73
  Listbox 73
  Menu 73, 74
  Menubutton 74
  Message 74
  OptionMenu 74
  Scale 75
  Spinbox 75
**address**
  generating 60
**apt-cache search &lt;keywords&gt; command 15**

## B

**base64 method 61**
**basic labels 66**
**buttonpressed function 47**
**buttons**
  adding 39-41

## C

**canvasclick function 64, 66**
**cd &lt;directory name&gt; command 14**

**center=location 59**
**character**
  creating 23, 24
  flight, controlling 30
  launching 28
  moving 26
**character, moving**
  initialization 26, 27
  keyboard, using 27, 28
**Checkbutton, widgets 72, 73**
**code blocks**
  about 22, 23
  URL 22
**code listing 69-71**
**command line, Raspberry Pi 13, 14**
**complete code listing 50**
**controller**
  using 46, 47
**controller base 39**
**count function 44**

## E

**Edit button 25**
**extensions**
  about 35, 71
  layout 72
  widgets 72

## F

**flight**
  controlling 30
**format function 60**
**format=type (optional) 59**
**Frame, widgets 73**

## G

**game**
  coding 45
  ending 32
**game, coding**
  controller, using 46, 47
  random module 45, 46
  time limit, adding 48
**game controller**
  buttons, adding 39-41
  controller base 39
  creating 38
  Raspberry Pi, connecting 42
**general purpose input/output (GPIO) 42**
**getmap function 61-64**
**Google Maps**
  about 59
  URL 59
**graphical user interface (GUI) 55**
**gravity**
  adding 31

## H

**Hello world!**
  about 21, 22
  program, writing 56, 57
  Tkinter 56

## I

**image**
  downloading 61
  using 62
**inputs, peripherals 7**

## K

**keyboard**
  used, for creating controller 52
  using 27, 28

## L

**LabelFrame, widgets 73**
**labels, adding**
  basic labels 66

  pop-up windows 66
**layout 72**
**level**
  creating 25, 26
**Listbox, widgets 73**
**ls command 13**

## M

**man <program name> command 14**
**map**
  address, generating 60
  Google Maps 59
  image, downloading 61
  image, using 62, 63
  obtaining 58
**maptype=type (optional) 59**
**markers, adding**
  mouse clicks, detecting 64
  mouse clicks, reacting to 64
**materials**
  for creating controller 37
**Menubutton, widgets 74**
**Menu, widgets 73, 74**
**Message, widgets 74**
**mouse clicks**
  detecting 64
  reacting to 64

## N

**network, peripherals 8**
**nexttarget function 46**
**NOOBS**
  URL 8

## O

**OptionMenu, widgets 74**

## P

**physics, adding**
  bouncing 31
  game, ending 32
  gravity 31
**play function 48, 49**
**pop-up windows 66**

power supply, peripherals 6
program
  writing 56, 57
Python
  about 43-45
  URL 44, 59

# R

Radiobutton, widgets 75
random module 45, 46
Raspberry Pi
  connecting to 42
  starting up 10-12
  troubleshooting 16
  uses 15
  using 13
Raspberry Pi forums
  URL 16
Raspberry Pi, peripherals
  inputs 7
  network 8
  power supply 6
  storage 6
  video 7
Raspberry Pi, using
  command line 13, 14
  new software, installing 14, 15
  new software, updating 14, 15
Raspberry Pi verified peripherals
  URL 6

# S

Scale, widgets 75
scoring 33, 34
Scratch
  about 20, 21
  code blocks 22, 23
  Hello world! 21, 22
  URL 20
SD card
  preparing 8, 9
SD Formatter
  URL 8
sensor=true/false 59

size=widthxheight 59
software
  installing 14, 15
  updating 14, 15
Spinbox, widgets 75
sprite 21
storage, peripherals 6
StringVar variable 73, 74
sudo command 15, 50

# T

Tab 14
time limit
  adding 48
Tkinter
  about 56
  URL 71
troubleshooting, Raspberry Pi 16

# U

Uniform Resource Locator (URL) 61

# V

video, peripherals 7

# W

widgets 56

# Z

zoom=value 59

## Thank you for buying
# Raspberry Pi Projects for Kids

# About Packt Publishing

Packt, pronounced 'packed', published its first book "*Mastering phpMyAdmin for Effective MySQL Management*" in April 2004 and subsequently continued to specialize in publishing highly focused books on specific technologies and solutions.

Our books and publications share the experiences of your fellow IT professionals in adapting and customizing today's systems, applications, and frameworks. Our solution based books give you the knowledge and power to customize the software and technologies you're using to get the job done. Packt books are more specific and less general than the IT books you have seen in the past. Our unique business model allows us to bring you more focused information, giving you more of what you need to know, and less of what you don't.

Packt is a modern, yet unique publishing company, which focuses on producing quality, cutting-edge books for communities of developers, administrators, and newbies alike. For more information, please visit our website: www.packtpub.com.

# About Packt Open Source

In 2010, Packt launched two new brands, Packt Open Source and Packt Enterprise, in order to continue its focus on specialization. This book is part of the Packt Open Source brand, home to books published on software built around Open Source licences, and offering information to anybody from advanced developers to budding web designers. The Open Source brand also runs Packt's Open Source Royalty Scheme, by which Packt gives a royalty to each Open Source project about whose software a book is sold.

# Writing for Packt

We welcome all inquiries from people who are interested in authoring. Book proposals should be sent to author@packtpub.com. If your book idea is still at an early stage and you would like to discuss it first before writing a formal book proposal, contact us; one of our commissioning editors will get in touch with you.

We're not just looking for published authors; if you have strong technical skills but no writing experience, our experienced editors can help you develop a writing career, or simply get some additional reward for your expertise.

## Instant Raspberry Pi Gaming

ISBN: 978-1-78328-323-1          Paperback: 60 pages

Your guide to gaming on the Raspberry Pi, from classic arcade games to modern 3D adventures

1. Learn something new in an Instant! A short, fast, focused guide delivering immediate results.

2. Play classic and modern video games on your new Raspberry Pi computer.

3. Learn how to use the Raspberry Pi app store.

4. Written in an easy-to-follow, step-by-step manner that will have you gaming in no time.

## Raspberry Pi Networking Cookbook

ISBN: 978-1-84969-460-5          Paperback: 204 pages

An epic collection of practical and engaging recipes for the Raspberry Pi!

1. Learn how to install, administer, and maintain your Raspberry Pi.

2. Create a network fileserver for sharing documents, music, and videos.

3. Host a web portal, collaboration wiki, or even your own wireless access point.

4. Connect to your desktop remotely, with minimum hassle.

Please check **www.PacktPub.com** for information on our titles

## Raspberry Pi Home Automation with Arduino

ISBN: 978-1-84969-586-2          Paperback: 176 pages

Automate your home with a set of exciting projects for the Raspberry Pi!

1.  Learn how to dynamically adjust your living environment with detailed step-by-step examples.

2.  Discover how you can utilize the combined power of the Raspberry Pi and Arduino for your own projects.

3.  Revolutionize the way you interact with your home on a daily basis.

## Raspberry Pi for Secret Agents

ISBN: 978-1-84969-578-7          Paperback: 152 pages

Turn your Raspberry Pi into your very own secret agent toolbox with this set of exciting projects!

1.  Detect an intruder on camera and set off an alarm.

2.  Listen in or record conversations from a distance.

3.  Find out what the other computers on your network are up to.

4.  Unleash your Raspberry Pi on the world.

Please check **www.PacktPub.com** for information on our titles

Made in the USA
Middletown, DE
28 December 2014